MW01280104

Born Again
AT THE
Laundromat

Born Again

AT THE

Laundromat

AND OTHER VISIONS
OF THE NEW WEST

▲

DaVe CARTY

LYONS & BURFORD, PUBLISHERS

Copyright © 1992 by Dave Carty

ALL RIGHTS RESERVED. No part of this book may be reproduced in any manner without the express written consent of the publisher, except in the case of brief excerpts in critical reviews and articles. All inquiries should be addressed to: Lyons & Burford, 31 West 21 Street, New York, NY 10010.

Poems by Paul Zarzysky and Wally McRae appearing in "Cowboy Poetry" are reproduced courtesy of the authors.

Designed by Catherine Lau Hunt

Printed in the United States of America

10   9   8   7   6   5   4   3   2   1

Library of Congress Cataloging-in-Publication Data

Carty, Dave.
    Born again at the laundromat : visions of the New West / Dave Carty.
        p.   cm.
    ISBN 1-55821-200-0
    1. West (U.S.)—Social life and customs. 2. Carty, Dave.
I. Title.
F595.3.C36   1992
978—dc20   92-25180
                                                                CIP

FOR MY MOTHER AND GRANDMOTHER

Contents

INTRODUCTION

Funny how the mind works. After the six months and fifty thousand words it took to produce this book, I've been asked by my publisher to write a two-page introduction, and I can't think of a damn thing to say.

Perhaps a recounting of history will suffice. Several years ago, somewhat jaded by the magazine articles I write for a living, I decided to compile a collection of my essays—which, then as now, were often as not pieces I'd written that no one would even look at, much less buy. The one publisher who expressed interest in the project backed out after I simply could not give the collection a unifying theme. And that was the end of that.

So I put the essays on a back burner and wrote a novel. The novel didn't sell either; still hasn't sold, in fact, and some have assured me that it never will. We shall see. Meanwhile, several of the essays from my long-dead collection were circulating around New York City, and eventually ended up in publisher Peter Burford's hands. He wrote me a short (two paragraph) letter wondering if I'd be interested in putting together a book of similar pieces, no theme required. For this stroke of luck I credit clean living, due in large part to the lack of means that would enable me to live any other way.

1

Writers—at least those who write essays and fiction—write because they enjoy it, no matter what they say on talk radio. On that note, I'd like to take this opportunity to apologize to the people I've bored over the years with my tales of poverty and editorial incompetence. I had fun with this, though I still can't find a unifying theme to it all, as hard as I've looked.

Dave Carty
Bozeman, Montana
April, 1992

DEAD SKUNKS AND WHY

This spring it happened again. Several thousand courageous but stupid skunks died while crossing Montana highways, Rorschach ink blots on an asphalt cue card. Their lemminglike single-mindedness is to be pondered, if not admired. After skirting several hundred carcasses over the course of last May and June, I couldn't help but wonder why the hell they did it.

Skunks aren't the only casualties, of course. Pheasants, Richardson's ground squirrels, and deer—especially deer—contribute their share of gore to roadside landscapes. Skunks alone, however, seem bent on self-imposed genocide. But that's what you get for playing chicken with two tons of accelerating underbody. The toughest skunk in town isn't tougher than the oil pan of a Ford 150.

Although I didn't keep tabs, there seemed to be more than the usual amount of carnage last year, as there had been three years before. Then, the deceased lay like throw rugs across every other mile of Interstate 90. The following spring's kills, however, seemed moderate. I thought that year's low body count might indicate that all the suicides had done themselves in the year before. When a second nonsanguinary spring passed, I hoped for the best; maybe they'd gotten a handle on their problem. But I was wrong. They were back in '88. It turned out that 1988 was a good year for skunks. Or a bad year, if you happened to be a skunk on a Montana road.

Examine any road-killed skunk in the state, and what you'll find is what used to be a black, cat-sized animal with two broad white stripes that run the length of either side of the body, converging briefly on the rump before splaying out

5

again to fringe both sides of a handsome, squirrel-like tail. With no small inspiration, biologists have dubbed these animals *striped* skunks, and they're by far the most common species in the United States. They're pretty things, verging on cute, and if it weren't for the smell you might be tempted to pick one up, to cuddle it on your lap. De-scented, they make tractable pets, although their obtuse personalities have probably prevented them from barnstorming the pet-store circuit. I've yet to meet a tame skunk, but I've met plenty of wild ones, which have the charm and vigor of parking meters. To striped skunks, road kill may be the natural culmination of a ho-hum life style, much the same as a factory drone who, stuck in a put-the-wing-nut-on-the-screw job, drinks himself to death on weekends. Only quicker.

Despite their broad range, striped skunks aren't prolific breeders. The female gives birth to four to seven kits in late May, though a second litter is sometimes born later in the year. The young are born hairless and blind, but within six to eight weeks leave home (often an abandoned fox or woodchuck den or even a culvert), an event marked by an odd ritual, which George Whitney, a veterinarian who raised skunks, described in a 1986 issue of Yale University's *Discovery* magazine: "Immediately upon leaving the burrow, the kits form a circle, heads toward the center, and back in and out several times, after which they line up and follow their mother." Whitney's animals were caged, but had they been free to go, they no doubt would have beelined for the nearest blacktop. And the huddle? A pregame ritual, a prayer. Whitney offered no explanation. Animal behaviorists take note.

Striped skunks have poor vision at best, not surprising for

an animal with few natural enemies; they don't have to watch where they're going because only cars refuse to get out of their way. And although their odor makes them nearly invincible, nature has chinked that armor with disease: tularemia, Q fever, canine hepatitis, canine distemper, listeriosis, histoplasmosis, pleuritis, rabies—the list goes on, and it's not a pretty one. Furthermore, as if the roster of diseases wasn't enough, skunks must also deal with parasites, one of which is apropos of this discussion: nematodes.

I'm serious about this. Nematodes—parasitic worms—infest the sinuses of the animals, causing frontal lesions of the cranium. As a result, the cranium "downwarps" (a *Canadian Journal of Zoology* term, which apparently means "collapses," though I couldn't find a definition in either of the dictionaries I own), and the skunks suffer pressure on the brain. Scant research has been done on just how downwarping craniums affect skunks, but you can take it from me it doesn't make them feel like dancing. My unscientific opinion is that they lose their grip on the routine, as would anyone else with a downwarped cranium. They go bonkers—you know, lie around the burrow and twitch, stare at the ceiling. So now you have an animal that sees poorly, hears worse, is afraid of nothing, and is stupid *and* crazy. No wonder they're taking on Detroit.

I have yet to hit a skunk, although there are plenty in the state to choose from. They're nocturnal animals and don't get around much during the day. I'm a diurnal animal and don't get around much at night, so we have reached an unspoken agreement—I won't flatten them if they'll leave me and my dogs in peace. There have been breaches of trust. During a bow hunt last September, I had no sooner entered my ground blind

7

when a skunk marched in after me. I was hemmed in by silver buffalo-berry bushes, the skunk blocking my only exit. One simply does not run through silver buffalo-berrybushes—with their six-penny, concertina-wire thorns—any more than one runs through the turbines at Hoover Dam. But one considers it. The skunk ignored me, however, and waddled away.

And the individuals that my Brittany spaniel, Fancy, has pointed have all been remarkably tolerant, rocking from foot to foot while backing in the opposite direction. Each time, I've managed to grab her before the shooting started. So no, I haven't hit one yet. I leave them alone.

Still, for an animal that is rarely seen in daylight, it always surprises me that so many clutter the highways each morning. It's not like there aren't other places they could go. But Dennis Flath, a nongame coordinator with the Montana Department of Fish, Wildlife, and Parks, has a theory. Flath, incidentally, is the man who informed me that I was seeing striped skunks, not common skunks, as I had supposed. "Striped skunks," he said. "*Mephitis mephitis.*"

"Methodist Methodist?"

"No, no. Not Methodist Methodist. *Mephitis mephitis.*" Flath continued. "The striped skunk has a very effective defense mechanism."

"Not on cars," I said.

"No. But the species can defend itself quite well without having to run away from anything. Their scent can turn a coyote or almost any other predator around in a big hurry. But they haven't adapted to the presence of automobiles. They're actually a rather successful animal, behaviorally speaking, but they need more time to learn to deal with cars."

"Say . . ."

"A hundred thousand years ought to do it. Quite frankly, skunks have not yet learned to get out of the way."

Sadly, the little ones are usually the first to not get out of the way, and the survivors are no wiser for the experience. Should they live the year and weather the onslaught of Buicks and raptors (great horned owls are their only serious predators), chances are the females will return to the highways the following spring, another litter of shuffling targets in tow. There's no rhyme or reason to it; Flath discounts my nematode theory and says that skunks cross roads simply to reach the other side.

Short of bolting a stuffed owl to your grille, there isn't much you can do to avoid hitting one eventually. They're night roamers, and the night is dark. Skunks are black. *Splat.* At seventy-five you can't swerve (everybody goes seventy-five in Montana). *Splat.* Maybe you *like* to hit skunks. People have prejudices, you know. Take cats, for instance. Take miniature poodles. Take childproof aspirin bottles.

I have no solutions. Should you encounter a skunk waddling down the interstate some evening and manage to avoid it, you can be certain that the next car will do the job right, and you'll have to plow through the mess on your way home. Unlike deer crossings, skunk crossings are not marked. And why should they be? Skunks are too blind to read.

As Flath says, maybe someday they'll learn. Maybe it won't take a hundred thousand years. Maybe it will dawn on them, someday, that *we don't have to do this anymore.* Maybe.

But probably not.

9

PHOTO NERDS
FROM HELL

We're in our twenties and early thirties—old men in a college town. So in the winter we bowl. Denver, Jeff, Woody (the Woodman), Dale, and Roper are charter members. I'm a substitute, but since someone fails to show every Thursday, I've become a regular. I'm the only non-photographer in the group; we're the Photo Nerds From Hell. Our rallying cry: *They stooped to conquer, and they brought their balls with them.*

The truth is that only Woody, Denver, and Jeff have the slightest notion of how to play the game. My previous experience, consisting of one or two evenings every couple of years, has hardly prepared me for this, a serious winter league with serious bowlers. Our competitors are sponsored by Kenyon Noble Lumber and Ace Hardware and wear navy-blue bowling shirts with their nicknames embroidered across the back. Also, they're good and we're not. Drink reinforces my opinion of the sport; as we drain pitchers of beer my scores and respect for the game decline apace. I've always considered bowling a ludicrously inane pastime, on a par with one-legged sack races and shot-putting. But fun.

Jeff and Woody have custom balls given to them by their wives. Woody's ball has "Woodman" engraved below the thumb hole, a homey touch. Tonight, Denver and Dale and I, lacking wives and custom balls, pick through the rental racks at the alley. While I stroll along the three-tiered shelves, slipping my thumb and middle fingers into holes and wondering what exactly a properly fitting ball feels like, Denver and Dale make selections and leave. Denver has found the same ball he used the week before, a former custom job that also has a name engraved below the thumb hole: "Denny." Did

Denny abandon his plain black ball for a snazzy, marbled-red AMF Brunswick? I wonder.

We're bowling in lane eight. Denver, Dale, Jeff, and Woody are bowling practice frames when I stagger up with my 200-pound prize, a corroded black orb with finger holes the size of Corvette exhaust ports. "For a smoother delivery, Carty likes 'em loose," the endorsements in *Bowlers Journal* will read. On my first try I manage to level three pins, which is thirty percent of the available pins, which gives me a 300 batting average. Not bad for a hack.

We're surrounded by men in rayon shirts and pebble-grain bowling shoes. Many wear wrist braces that remind me of the forearm pads worn by football linemen. I can't imagine what they're for, but I like their dark looks. I envision myself in a matched pair, one set for dress, one for casual wear.

Our first pitcher of beer is already gone, so Denver summons the waitress. She's a sweet old gal, thirtyish, with the graceful neck of a heron and a patient smile. Her hairstyle says native Montanan, raised up in Wolf Point country. She asks, "You boys ready for another?" And we rain dollar bills upon the table in reply. "Right back," she says.

In the next lane over are the Legionnaires, a group of spry oldsters well into their eighties. One totters to the foul line cradling a ball on his hip, squints at the pins, then rocks his pelvis forward and ejects the ball at his feet, backpedaling dramatically. The ball wobbles down the alley, while the man sways in the throes of body English. Eventually, the ball leans into the headpin and pushes it over, and a moment later the surrounding pins topple and fall. A strike. He shuffles back to his table and, seeing me watching, winks.

We're a diverse lot. Jeff is a film developer by trade, but his bowling background is more obscure. He's a six-footer like me, but heavier, solid. Jeff's a power bowler, and his ball cracks into the pins like a rifle shot. His muscular style elicits awe from team members and bystanders alike. How can anyone hurl a sixteen-pound ball that hard? He's got a 140 average, and he and Denver are responsible for the team's middling position in the league standings; without their scores the rest of us would settle like river mud to the bottommost layer of mediocrity.

Denver is our high-point man, but on his first frame he lodges his thumb in the ball and is yanked into the lane, scratching, while the rest of us shriek hysterically. That Denver. He and Dale are free-lance photographers, both working professionals. Denver's specialty is wildlife; Dale's is outdoor sports. Both make good livings selling pictures to national magazines, which means that they don't have to depend on the dismal Montana economy for work.

Since Dale will soon marry, we take pains to illuminate the bachelor life. Behind us two coeds cruise the rental racks, and I thump Dale in the ribs. The shorter girl is round, the taller one leggy and olive skinned. Both are blond and sport the post–Farrah Fawcett tresses fashionable among Montana State sororities. They're working their way through the rows of balls, delicately slipping tanned fingers in and out of finger holes. When the taller girl leans over the rack, Dale groans. By the time they glide back to their table, heads down, every man in the room is watching.

Odds are that these are ranch kids—cowgirls who grew up goat roping and barrel racing, whose raw-cheeked, leatherassed daddies would as soon dry gulch a city boy as talk to one who looked at his daughter that way. Years earlier, a potential dalliance with one such youngster had vaporized when her mother informed me that her daughter had left town indefinitely to "help move the cows out of the high pasture." These girls spend their formative years in Malta and Judith Gap, then enroll at the state universities in Missoula and Bozeman for schooling and a taste of city life. For many, college is an expansive dawn. They graduate with degrees in English or history, find teaching jobs in the Midwest, and leave. The rest marry rodeo-club sweethearts and move back to the ranch.

Evidently, our diversion with the coeds has improved our second game. That's not surprising considering we've had the first game as a warm-up; quite surprising considering the amount of beer we've drunk. In the first frame, Denver and Jeff roll spares, and Woody, with his proper, upright form, rolls a strike. Even I'm doing better; I knock down seven pins with my first ball.

As I wait by the ball return, the tall blond steps to the line two lanes down. Next I hear the ripping-canvas sound of chairs skidding across short-napped carpeting, and suddenly the Photo Nerds are on their feet, staring. Now she steps forward, bowls, and slinks back to her table, arms fixed against her sides. The Photo Nerds return to their seats, and Dale orders a pitcher. The girls' boyfriends glare. But we are not abased, for lo, we are the guys, and this is our night out.

Our scores decline in the final set. As one of two consummate novices (Dale is the other), mine slides the most. The Woodman, critiquing from the table, offers advice. "Keep

16

your back straight, Dave," he tells me. He stands to demonstrate. "Back straight, stiff wrist, follow through."

"Oh," I say. Why hasn't he told me this before? From now on I'll bowl properly, but the forced improvements are awkward and I soon revert to my old form, which, though a mockery of the art, at least feels good. My score for the final game is 98, an unapproachable dead last for the evening. Jesus.

"I need water. Could you get me some water please?" Dale is speaking into the microphone to the bartender, leaving Jeff, Roper, Woody, and me wedged against the counter at the Hauf Brau, a downtown bar. Nobody is thinkng about bowling; instead we gape in astonishment as Dale plays harmonica with the house band. He's into it; he scowls and grinds his foot into the floor, knee pumping, and during the chorus he dips his harp in a glass of water and curls around the mike, sings them low-down blues. Nobody knew he could do this.

Musical talent in others instantly arouses my envy. I cannot sing or play an instrument, yet fantasies of rock stardom persist at age thirty-three. The audience is giving it back to Dale, and he finishes the set howling into the microphone. When he was a fishing guide, he later admits, he jammed with Asleep at the Wheel, the rock and blues band, in West Yellowstone. "Man! Y'all blow a mane harp," says Roper, late of Jackson, Mississippi. "I'm gonna buy y'all bare."

Once we find a table, Jeff counts heads for next week's game. We're going to be shorthanded; Dale is flying to Connecticut for his wedding. But I'll bowl, and Roper and Woody

17

will be there too. Yet Woody fidgets. He's unhappy with his average, which has dropped to 115.

"Hell, Woody," I tell him, "I bowled a 98 tonight."

"But I'm a 130 bowler," he says, smiling strangely.

"You're having a slump."

"I've been having a slump all year."

"You'll do better next week."

"I may not come next week."

"You're a Photo Nerd from Hell and we need you."

"Right. This is no fun anymore."

I look at Jeff, but Jeff shrugs. Apparently, those with engraved bowling balls are serious about their sport. The following Thursday, the Woodman shows just long enough to tell us all that he's out of there for good.

No smile brightens the Olympic bowler's bearded face. He strides to the return and cups spindly hands over the air vents, then steps to the foul line, solemnly lifting his ball heavenward, left elbow awry, eyes straight ahead. Blue light dances along his wrist brace.

Now he lowers the ball, and then it's behind him and he's moving, and then come the four quick steps. Gently, oh! Gently the ball kisses the lane and is curving, curving away. It flirts with the gutter but breaks at last and angles into the pins, two of which fall. The Olympic bowler adjusts his pink baseball cap and waits for the second frame.

The Olympic bowler was the Woodman's favorite punching bag. "That guy really sucks," Woody delighted in saying. The man's style is almost effeminate in its perfection, and it is for this alone that Woody coined the nickname. It's true that the

Olympic bowler is no prodigy, though he's no worse than me. Tonight, however, without Woody to focus our attention, the Olympic bowler's posturing escapes the usual smirking commentary from our table. We're all edgy; Woody's exit has left us a man short and $6.50 shy of the weekly fee. Fortunately, the four of us can still play by deducting ten points from Woody's average and adding his adjusted score to each game's total. Woody's overall average, it turns out, really is 130, which is good news—even with the ten-point deduction, it's unlikely that any of our substitutes would have scored as well.

Competing against us tonight are the usual teams: the Olympic bowler's squad, who like us are in their twenties and early thirties, a carefree lot (with the exception of the Olympic bowler), though serious about the game if their custom shoes and wrist braces are any indication; a group of ranchers, windburned and purse lipped; and the Ace Hardware boys, middle-aged men in blue bowling shirts and Vitalis, upon one of whom falls the task of collecting the nightly fee. He's making the rounds now, a balding man with bifocals and a watermelon belly. When he reaches our table Jeff says, "Bob, we're a man short tonight."

"Well, I still need the $6.50." Bob makes a pistol with his finger and fist and pushes his glasses up his nose with the barrel. Jeff stares at him for a moment and then shakes down the rest of us for cash. Roper and Denver contribute two dollars, and Jeff and I put in a buck each. Bob glances at the money. "I need fifty cents," he says.

Jeff says, "Who's got fifty cents?" We reach into our pockets and shower pennies and nickles on the table. Jeff scoops them up, drops them in an envelope, and hands it to Bob. Bob leaves.

19

By the second game of the night we're hot. Denver, Jeff, and Roper are on fire; even I'm holding my own. Roper throws a strike and cuts loose with a rebel yell; in the ensuing round of team handshakes (a high five followed by the mimed tripping of a camera shutter) I forget alley protocol and bowl out of turn, crowding the Ace Hardware bowler in the next lane over. By the time I finish, Denver has turned his back to their table. "You better apologize to that guy," he says. The Ace Hardware bowler, a stork of a man with a Henry Kissinger pompadour, is glaring at me. I mouth "sorry" and shrug inanely. Me big stupido.

But in the mounting excitement it's hard to feel contrite, and with my scores soaring I fight the urge to showboat. What I want to do, what I *really* want to do, is mimic the choreographed, manicured form of the Olympic bowler. But he sits ten feet away, watching, and may be violent. His type often is.

By the beginning of the third game we have pulled ahead of Ace Hardware, a first. And then I see a curious thing: Behind our table, a man in a white dinner jacket shoves an overweight brunette and is instantly clubbed in the ear by the brunette's boyfriend. The man drops to the floor, rises, and staggers off mumbling, blood dribbling from his ear and puddling on the lapel of his jacket. The boyfriend follows while the woman leans against the rental counter and sobs. This goes on for ten minutes—the man staggering around the room, the boyfriend stalking at oblique angles. When the path of one crosses that of the other, words and punches are traded before bystanders can pull them apart. The police are not summoned and the two won't leave; it's thirty below outside and conceivable that the cold could kill them both.

20

When they finally retire to their corners the alley is buzz-
ing, but the surge of adrenaline only improves our scores.
Denver is closing on 200 in the ninth frame, and Roper and
Jeff aren't far behind. I'm still last, but for once relaxed and
confident. I bowl a strike in the ninth frame, and again in the
tenth, and then *again*, and then it's over. I've scored 159, my
best ever or since, and when the overhead monitor displays
our score we learn we've set a league high. Bob pushes his
glasses up his nose and strides over to congratulate us, and
Henry Kissinger shakes my hand.

In March the snow melts, and substitutes are hard to come
by. Dale's back, married now, but Woody has disappeared for
good, and though there are still six weeks left in the league,
the rest of us are looking forward to spring and fly-fishing.
The nights are warmer; no good for bowling. Despite our
league high, we bow out of the league dead last and two
weeks later are banned from all further competition for fail-
ure to give sufficient notice.

"Sufficient notice of what?" I ask Denver, who rolls his eyes
and shrugs.

"Banned for life," he says in an Orson Welles baritone.

As I walk to a convenience store the following morning, a
man approaches from the opposite direction. At a hundred
yards I recognize the beard and pink cap; it's the Olympic
bowler. But before I can say hello he turns up an alley, and
when I see him next his back is to me, gaze fixed, marching
grimly away. So: He's heard.

MISSOURI
BREAKS

Mark Batchelor is something of an anomaly. In Montana, a state in which the intrinsic value of wildlife is based on its palatability, Mark is a bird-watcher and an amateur naturalist, a local boy who rarely hunts. So when he asked that we beach our canoe an hour into a three-day float trip through Montana's Missouri River Breaks, I wasn't surprised.

Mark had seen—or thought he'd seen—a willet, a leggy shorebird he wanted to add to his life list. Our canoe thumped into shore, and my three-month-old Brittany spaniel, Fancy, somersaulted out of the bow and onto her head. For the remainder of the trip, she would not make a single graceful exit.

The bird had sprinted up a gravel bar, where it feigned indifference to our presence. "Gray legs or yellow legs?" Mark asked me, handing me his binoculars.

"Look gray to me."

That seemed to satisfy him. "It is a willet then," he said. And so it was. A moment later the bird wheeled away, and its white wing bars clinched Mark's identification.

We decided to have lunch (cheese, crackers, peanut butter, apples, and Ranier beer), and while we ate, Fancy pointed a cowbird. "Look," I whispered, "she's pointing."

"She's not moving," Mark said.

"That's a point." "Hey, that's great, really great," Mark said, without conviction. Mark has never hunted over a bird dog.

"That was her first one," I said, taking a final bite out of my apple. I gulped down the beer and tossed the apple core into the canoe. Already, it looked like a fine trip.

*   *   *

The Breaks do not suffer fools lightly. The next gravel road, should you be so reckless as to break an axle on the last, is a hot and dusty two-days' walk away. The river, it is easy to imagine, has changed little since Captains Meriwether Lewis and William Clark pushed through in the summer of 1805, dragging loaded freight canoes *upstream* behind them.

But the river has changed. Besides the abandoned homesteads on the banks and the long-buried wrecks of steamboats on the bottom, the Missouri has been plugged by massive Fort Peck Reservoir Dam, some two hundred miles downstream of tiny Virgelle, Montana. Still, the White Cliffs area, a half-day's float below our departure point at Coalbanks Landing, is largely pristine. And on any weekend save those in the proximity of Memorial Day, the Fourth of July, or Labor Day, the river is deserted.

Mark and I went on Memorial Day.

Don Sorenson, a free-lance pharmacist, shuttle driver, and antique dealer who owns the Virgelle Mercantile in Virgelle (the Virgelle Mercantile *is* Virgelle), had warned us that the river would be crowded. But Mark's schedule wouldn't permit another time slot, so off we went, along with a hundred other canoeists, incipient sunstroke victims, and blotto office workers. Among the dozen or so parties we saw launching from Coalbanks, only a handful had stashed fishing rods. That was fine with me—if I was going to paddle into the bowels of the Missouri Breaks for the weekend, I'd just as soon have ten or twelve miles of river to fish by myself.

The upper Missouri is home to a number of warm-water fish: sturgeon, goldeye shiners, northern pike, walleye, ling, drum, carp, paddlefish, channel cats—especially cats—and

26

even a few largemouth bass and brown trout. What I was not told, prior to our departure, was that there weren't a lot of any of them.

But wait. Don Sorenson *had* said something about that. Still, he figured we'd catch a few catfish if we worked at it, so I lashed a spinning rod to the thwarts, next to the extra paddle. And in keeping with the community spirit of things, Mark and I cracked beers as we shoved off.

The first mile's float below Coalbanks Landing was anything but lonely. Canoes were the most common craft, but we saw several kayaks, one driftboat, numerous rafts, a rowboat or two, and a pair of outboard- and canopy-equipped pontoon boats whose blitzed occupants thought my picture taking hilarious. Over the rumble of twin Mercs, one screamed at me, "Hey, you shooting this for a magazine?"

Most of the people we passed were novice paddlers, or novice drinkers, or both, and a stiff upstream wind made downstream progress all the more difficult. Mark and I had both paddled canoes before, and though neither of us was expert at it, we worked well together and had soon outdistanced the crowd.

Several hours later, the white sandstone cliffs for which this stretch of the Missouri is named appeared—low bluffs, then walls, spires, and ridges. One expanse of pale rock plunged into the water, and hundreds of cliff swallows were building nests on its face—a show that stopped every boat on the river. These were the same birds, Mark informed me, that returned yearly to Capistrano.

"Look at the mud daubers," said a woman's voice in a canoe behind us.

"They're *cliff* swallows," said Mark, who knows.

By late afternoon we'd covered eighteen miles and were ready to stop for the night. Mark suggested paddling to a grove on the south bank, another quarter-mile downstream. This we did.

While Fancy chased grasshoppers, Mark and I unloaded the canoe. We discovered that neither of us had packed a shovel, so Mark built an elaborate rock fire ring, and I scrubbed the parched surrounding soil clean of potential tinder. Fortunately, the wood we gathered was bone dry and virtually sparkless, and over a dinner of antelope steaks we began to relax.

In addition to the spinning rod, I had brought a sponge, a package of quarter-ounce egg sinkers, swivels, long-shanked size 2 hooks, anise oil, and two dozen night crawlers. I threaded my line through an egg sinker and tied it to a swivel, then added another foot of line, which I tied to a hook. Using a technique I'd learned as a kid in Iowa, I sliced off a chunk of sponge, threaded it onto the hook, and saturated it with anise oil. A night crawler followed that, and ten seconds later I had my first hit. Maybe ten seconds. It could have been sooner.

But whatever was on the end of my line was not a catfish. It fought like a trout, and after my first glimpse of its silvery flanks, that's what I thought it was. Yet what I soon held flopping in my hand was like no fish I had ever seen. Save for eyes the size and color of Krugerrands, the ten-inch fish had the pearly lines of a baby tarpon and the channel-lock jaws of a piranha. It was the first goldeye shiner I took on our trip, but not the last; I caught another on my next cast. In fact, I caught goldeyes on every cast, and it quickly became apparent that I would not be catching a catfish any time soon, what with the goldeyes filching my worms before the sinker hit bottom. Sorenson, I then remembered, had told me to use a goldeye for bait. So I killed one and cut strips of leathery flesh from its back and sides. Rebaiting thus accomplished, I squatted on the bank and dug through my gear for the eighty-pound-test dacron line in my gear bag.

Up to six trotlines with six hooks on each are allowed in the Breaks, although I used just one line. On each hook I threaded a sponge and then a wedge of shiner meat. I weighted the line with a two-ounce sinker, then swung it bolo style over my head and flung it, on my second try, into the river. On my first try, one of the anise oil and shiner-meat embellished number 2 hooks sank into the tip of my thumb.

According to my newly bloodstained regulations, there was no limit on sturgeon, catfish, burbot (ling), and most other nongame fish in that stretch of the Missouri. As far as the sturgeon went, that seemed a moot point: Nobody we talked to had ever caught one. Nor would the catfish play ball. An hour after my last cast, Mark and I sat by the fire and watched my unmoving rod. Then Mark said, "There's a truck across the river."

In the near dark, twin beams bounced along the bank, stopped, and crept forward again. I wondered if these were BLM rangers, come to douse our puny fire and haul us away. The lights winked off, doors opened, and waves of rock and roll thumped across the chill river air. Mark lifted his binoculars. "They're not rangers," he said. There was a faint clang of galvanized tin, followed by a muffled whoosh as flames erupted from the river bank, instantly illuminating a half dozen spectral figures setting up tents and gathering wood. After a day's paddle into the heart of the wilderness, misfortune had dumped a squad of philistines in our laps.

Fifteen minutes later, Mark asked me why my rod was doing that.

"Doing what?"

"Pointing downstream and all bent over like that."

I jumped to my feet, yanked the rod off the bank and set the hook. But aside from the bend in the rod, there was no movement, nothing to indicate a fish on the end of the line. Yet there was something down there, and as I pumped and reeled, Mark gestured. "It's a catfish!" he said, pointing at the water. And it was, too. The fish weighed five or six pounds, and aside from being the first cat I'd taken from the Missouri, it was the largest I'd caught anywhere, ever. The big cat went on a stringer and we went to bed, and at five o'clock the next morning the shooting started.

I hadn't expected that. The crack of the first shot slapped me awake as though with the flat of a canoe paddle. Fancy bolted to her feet. The next shot sent a geyser of water spouting from shore two hundred yards upriver, followed by a curtain of spray as someone emptied the clip of a .22 semiautomatic. Bullets shrieked overhead.

After an hour of continuous explosions from rimfires and large-caliber rifles, the shooting stopped. Mark sensibly argued against a counterattack, reminding me that we hadn't brought guns. We decided to eat breakfast and leave immediately afterwards. I inspected the canoe and was relieved to discover that it had not taken enemy fire. More good news: The trotline attached to the bow was throbbing; a catfish, slightly smaller than the first, had swallowed one of the baits. That gave us two cats for breakfast, and while Mark built a fire, I cleaned the fish.

Although the Missouri may not hold large numbers of channel cats, the two we had that morning were the fattest, most delicious catfish I'd ever eaten. As table fare, catfish take a backseat to no other fish, including trout, which in my heretical opinion are vastly overrated. But our breakfast was marred when a delegation approached from the opposite bank.

There were three of them, all local high school kids. They were surprised we'd caught catfish, although they admitted they'd never fished this stretch before. They'd be floating the river for the next two days, the one sipping a Budweiser said. Mark and I attempted smiles. Small world. We'd be floating the next two days too.

When they left, their friends saluted their return by firing a round an oar's length in advance of their boat. Much laughter from the far shore. We threw our gear in the canoe and paddled away.

We saw no one else that morning. Stopping for lunch at a wide bend, we explored the ruins of a cabin built with logs that had been hauled into the treeless breaks—from where we could not determine. Prairie dogs chirped from crumbling warrens.

At four o'clock we established camp in a glade of cottonwoods. While Fancy scavenged for cow pies, I went fishing, but the water was shallow, and though goldeyes tugged at my bait, I was unable to hook one. The meat on the trotline was still usable, however, so I resaturated the sponges with anise oil and heaved the whole works into the river.

31

That night the wind bellowed, and sometime after midnight I scampered down the riverbank in my underwear, genuinely worried that the canoe would blow away. I spun the boat into the wind, grabbing the trotline—which I'd tied to the bow—as I did so. The line was tight and heavy. Yo! Catfish! You out there?

The following morning the wind abated somewhat, and after breakfast the procession of boats we'd passed the previous two days floated by, many now sporting makeshift sails. I took pictures and waved, then walked to the canoe and hauled in my line. The baits had not been touched.

On the paddle out, Fancy, who had been snoozing on a pile of duffel, awoke, saw a cliff swallow and, half asleep, tripped over the gunwale in pursuit and fell into the river. A lady in a passing canoe laughed out loud. "What a cute puppy," she said.

HOME
GAME

On the eve of October 11, Forsyth, Montana, is jumping. Men from all over the country—and a few wives and teenage sons—have converged on this one-horse farming town on the Yellowstone River for the opening of antelope season, now just two days away. Many eventually head north to the Reeves ranch, where Mrs. Reeves, a friendly, attractive lady in her fifties, collects a ten-dollar trespass fee per person for permission to hunt on her land. "It's good the entire season," she says, "and you can come back and hunt anytime you want."

Last year, she estimates that three hundred head of antelope were killed on her ranch, nearly all during the first week of the season. To that end, she collected fees from well over one hundred people. Mrs. Reeves is not one to let opportunity go knocking.

Earlier, when I had first spoken with her, I was the first hunter she'd seen that season. Certainly I could hunt on her place, she'd told me. "Expect company on opening day. Last year we had 150."

"One hundred and fifty *hunters*?"

"Yup," she said.

At the moment no one was in sight. It was hard to imagine this pitched, dry land hiding a battalion of riflemen and their balloon-tired ATVs, but Mrs. Reeves, I later learned, knew what she was talking about.

By noon I had found three bands of antelope, all with smallish bucks in tow. I had seen one good animal—fourteen, maybe fifteen inches, which had continued to stare at me even after I'd stopped, rolled down my truck window, and whistled at him from the road. But he was not on the Reeves ranch,

35

and the man whose land he was on charged a flat hundred-dollar trespass fee. No one in Montana pays a hundred dollars to shoot a "goat," including me. I drove on.

The next best buck I saw was running with a herd on a distant and separate section of Mrs. Reeves's land. Since the land was not connected to the main body of her ranch, I hoped the other 149 anticipated guests would overlook it. I eased down a dusty two-track that looped down and in, stopping at a stock tank that floated clots of dead algae. I could park my camper there the night before the season, out of sight of the antelope on the ridge above. In the meantime, I'd see if I could locate a better buck. And I'd spend tonight in town, closer to the bars.

Throughout October, Forsyth receives a caravan of Win-nebagos, minivans, and camper-towing Ford pickups, all of which gas up at the Town Pump on Main Street. I saw one colossus of a motor home with a pair of Honda trail bikes lashed to the grille, and later that afternoon watched through binoculars as their grim-faced riders saddled up and headed off into a red and western sunset, rifles in camo nylon scab-bards, the whine of two-stroke engines droning across a mile and a half of sagebrush.

Inside the store, the place was churning. Men in blaze-orange coats milled around the checkout stand, buying blaze-orange hats, Montana turd birds (a lacquered cow pie fitted with bead eyes and feathers—a trinket for the little woman), and boxes of .243 shells. The shells were cheap, but I was hoping I wouldn't need another box. Money was tight and I had half a box already; that would have to be enough. Instead,

36

I bought $1.59 worth of cheese nachos, which congealed in their cardboard tray while I waited, twitching, for whoever was in the rest room ahead of me to get the hell out of there.

"Can I help you?" It was one of the girls behind the counter. She was in her early twenties, and pretty in a way not out of character with her green polyester double knits.

"I'm waiting for the bathroom," I said. She smirked and handed me the keys.

Forsyth High School is four blocks north of the Burlington Northern tracks, set into an incline above the Yellowstone River. The Forsyth Dogies were recent Class B champs, and that evening they were playing the St. Labre Braves, a team from the Northern Cheyenne Indian Reservation that had not, in anyone's recent memory, ever won a football game. As I backed my camper into place, a man tapped on my window.

"You planning to spend the night here?" He had folded his jacket over his arms, and as I rolled down my window he plucked at the zipper.

"Is that all right?"

"It's not up to me. I mean, it's okay with me but I don't run this place. I just run the pool." He glanced over his shoulder at the semicircular brick building behind him. More fiddling with the zipper. "You'll have to talk to the cops. If it's okay with them, I guess it's okay with me."

"I'll do that," I said. He thanked me and walked off.

After dinner, I washed the dishes, hung the towel from a clothesline above the door, and cracked a Budweiser. Outside, gravel popped under the wheels of arriving cars. Shortly, the lights above the playing field blinked on one by one, illuminating knots of men in purple satin booster jackets.

When the Dogies jogged onto the field, I slipped into my parka and walked toward the bleachers. A cop parked at the entrance assured me that I could spend the night on the school lot. "All right by me," he said. "Did you talk to the guy who works at the pool?"

With five minutes remaining in the first half, Forsyth had rocketed to a 48 to 0 lead. The Braves couldn't muster enough players to run a separate offense and defense, and the team's tiny knot of boosters huddled against the visiting bleachers, warming to a pint of Yukon Jack. Across the field, the Forsyth coach, a ruddy-faced man in his late twenties, grinned and poked his assistants. When the half-time gun sounded, I left.

It's hard to discuss entertainment with locals without sounding like a lecher come to bother their girls, but that's closer to the truth than claiming you just want a quiet drink while surrounded by any and all available women. The clerk at the Town Pump told me to go to the Kokomo, which had hired a Billings band just for the opening of antelope season.

The place was empty when I arrived, but the band wasn't half bad. Two baby-faced high school kids—twins, it appeared—fronted a four-piece group that hammered out Chuck Berry tunes. I ordered a beer, drank it down, ordered another, and shoved it between my legs on the bar stool.

In this land where the sky is big, single women drive Nissan and Toyota sedans, and married women drive their husband's four-wheel-drive Ford pickups. Of course, this observation is worthless in a bar without windows. Three

38

HOME GAME

beers and a scotch later, the Kokomo had begun to fill, and every woman not within twelve inches of a man under a Stetson was single as far as I was concerned. One, a lithe six-footer in red heels, was making eye contact. The band broke into "Roll Over Beethoven," and as she jitterbugged across the dance floor I nearly swooned.

Within an hour the Kokomo was packed, and I was wedged against the bar. I recognized the Forsyth football coach standing with a group of boosters in purple jackets. "Hey," I said. "How'd you guys do?"

"We tried to call it at the half, but they scored once and wanted to keep playing." He smiled. "So we beat them 64 to 6."

"Those guys didn't look like they were really into it," I said.

"Nah, they really sucked. Drink?"

"Thanks, I've got one."

To my right, three men in motorcycle jackets cradled bottles of Coors. The smallest, a swarthy, balding man, was having an animated discussion with the bartender. "I want you out! Out of my bar," the bartender said. The man said something, and the bartender pointed toward the door. The man slammed his beer on the counter and stomped out.

The bartender saw me watching. "That son of a bitch," he said. "Shook up a beer and gave it to one of my best customers."

"You did what you had to do," I said.

"Every week it's the same thing. I ought to eighty-six his ass once and for all."

"Gotta run a business," I said.

39

An enormous, moon-faced woman was on my left, and sitting beside her a man my age was watching the woman in red heels. I ordered another drink.

Red heels was alone, her brunette hair swept to the side, her satin blouse shimmering in the aura of the Miller Highlife display. Her thin fingers flashed bands of gold and silver. A man in a crewneck sweater drifted across the room and slipped his arm around her waist, and she turned, smiling, and kissed him on the cheek. They spoke briefly, then separated. She glanced again in my direction, and my pulse surged.

"Say honey, you got a match?" It was the woman on my left.

"Sorry, I don't smoke," I said. I swung back toward the room, but above the thump of the band I heard a whimper, like the tremulous whine of a puppy. The fat woman beside me was crying. Big, plump tears rolled down her cheeks and puddled in the folds of her chin. I tried not to look at her.

"Would you hold my hand? Please?" She was sobbing. The bartender watched her carefully.

"Please?"

I extended my hand limply, like a rag on a stick. She shoved it in her lap, clutching my wrist fiercely.

But her tears stopped, and she rubbed her nose on her sleeve. "You all right?" she asked.

"I can't reach my drink."

"Why, honey?"

"You've got my hand."

She massaged my arm. "Want to dance?"

The bartender took a step toward her, then turned away.

"Might as well," I said. The competition was dancing with red heels, who towered over him. At maybe five-three, he couldn't have played football for Forsyth, ever. I thought about cutting in, although I'd never done it before and in fact didn't know if such things were still being done in eastern Montana. Once, a friend of mine had bought a drink for a woman he'd spotted across a bar, had it delivered by a deferential and anonymous bartender, just like in the movies. She had smiled and waved, and later they had left together. He told me everything.

I stepped away from the bar, my wrist still locked in the woman's grip. She slid from her stool, wobbled forward, and slumped into the two bikers, knocking one to the floor.

I backpedaled wildly. "It wasn't me!" I said.

The bartender rushed around the bar. "Irene, *you're drunk!*" Irene sat up, pouting. "We was dancing," she said, pointing at me. The bartender dragged her to her feet and propped her against the wall. The biker stood up and backed away. "I'm gonna have to cut you off, Irene," the bartender said. Irene's eyes pinched shut and she began to gurgle. "We was dancing," she said. I slipped into the crowd and made my way to the men's room.

Inside, I pressed my forehead against the wall above the urinal and watched the porcelain trough undulate around my legs. Behind me, a man combed his blond hair. "Where are *you* from?" he asked.

"Bozeman," I said.

"I figured you wasn't from around here. What are you doing in Forsyth?"

"Antelope hunting."

"You drove all the way from Bozeman to hunt antelope?" I
I admitted that I had, and he shook his head at the wonder of
it all. He said, "Want some advice?"

I said that I did.

"Call up John Krieger . . . you got a pencil?" I searched my
shirt for a pen, and he scribbled a number on one of his busi-
ness cards. "Call this guy. He used to be a game warden here,
and he knows where every damn antelope in the county
is. Tell him Rob from Forsyth Heating and Cooling sent
you."

"Well, I've already paid to hunt up on the Reeveses' place."

"Hell, you shouldn't have to pay to shoot no *goat*. Call him."

"Thanks, I will," I said.

Back on the dance floor, Irene was careening about with
her arm locked around the waist of one of the bikers. I ducked
behind a cluster of cowboys and edged to the bar. Someone
brushed my arm, and when I turned red heels was standing
beside me, speaking to the bartender.

"Hi," I said.

"Hello."

"Good band."

"Yeah. They're good."

"What's your name?"

"Lisa."

"Hi, Lisa," I said.

"Hi."

"Say, I was . . ."

"Well, gee. I've got to get back to my friend." She pushed
three dollars across the counter and walked away. "See you,"
she said. And she walked away.

42

When the bartender came by he frowned. "I'm glad you're out of that," he said, jerking his thumb at Irene, who by now had buried her face in the chest of her dance partner.

"What?"

"She's bad news," he said.

"Who?"

"Irene."

"Why?"

"Her husband shoots people."

"Oh."

"He's out of town this week, though." he said. "Need another drink?"

I shook my head, but he had walked away, and when he returned he had a beer in his hand. "It's on me," he said.

Red heels and her midget boyfriend were sitting at a table, talking.

The following morning I lurched into a telephone booth and dialed John Krieger's number. My head pulsed.

A woman answered. "Yes?"

"Hi. Is John Krieger there?"

"No, he's out of town. Who is this?"

"I'm a friend of Rob's . . . from Forsyth Heating and Cooling? You don't know me, but . . . John's not there? Rob told me he might be able to tell me where to find some antelope."

"John's not here," she said.

I said, "Thanks anyway," and hung up.

Late that afternoon I parked my camper by the stock tank. The wind had picked up, so I zipped my parka to my chin and walked over to the tank. Under a skiff of ice, water-boatmen kicked in torpid circles. That evening the wind died and eighteen Hungarian partridge (I counted) walked out of the sagebrush, clucking softly to themselves. On the ridge above me a herd of antelope browsed, and tomorrow was the first day of the season.

BORN
AGAIN
AT THE
LAUNDROMAT

D oes that great wrangler of lost souls, Jesus, summer
    on a dude ranch? Judging by the number of times
I've been waylaid by His disciples lately, I suspect He's got
irons in the fire somewhere around these parts. Or maybe I
simply look like I need help—not that I'm overly receptive to
advice from people who wear wool suits when it's pushing
ninety. In a perfect democracy, I'd be more tolerant, but I've
already gone a few rounds with the Lord, and come out look-
ing like lion bait.

In high school, I had a friend named Jason. Jason wasn't his
real name; like any good American, he'd probably sue me if I
identified him. Jason was strikingly handsome, a hot tennis
player for our high school team, and when he wasn't chasing
girls or playing tennis, he sold pot.

In the early seventies, selling pot wasn't a particularly un-
usual way for a seventeen-year-old to make spending money.
Jason sold and smoked enough to keep himself in a happy
stupor through a semester's worth of Algebra III, during
which he'd chortle more or less continually from the back of
the room. Our befuddled teacher's thick Okie drawl was the
usual precipitant: Mr. Jackson would stretch a vowel and Ja-
son would go to pieces.

Besides tennis, Jason's other significant talent was shop-
lifting. I remember seeing a pocket calculator he'd stolen, this
when pocket calculators wouldn't fit in a pocket and still cost
upwards of a hundred dollars. He knew how to evade most of
the electronic surveillance systems of the time and had a ga-
rage full of smoking merchandise to show for it.

One day, Jason and his fifteen-year-old brother ran away to
Canada, financing the trip with gasoline appropriated from

service stations. They were caught in Washington for a traffic violation ("That's what I get for letting my little brother drive," he told me), and returned to their parents. A year later, Jason went to college on a tennis scholarship, and sometime after that, threw it all out the window for another run at Canada. The way I heard it, he'd jumped bail on a drug bust.

I never saw him again. But a few years later, while having dinner with mutual friends, I got an update. Jason had become a Jehovah's Witness. "It's just weird," my friend told me. "We go over to his house and he sits around and reads the Bible. His wife too. You can't believe it's him." I doubt if anyone wants the old Jason back, gone in spirit now for nearly fifteen years. But heaven help me, the guy was fun to be around, even if he was crazy. Who knows? The new Jason may have been the Witness who wedged his toe in my door last winter. They tell me I wouldn't recognize him.

There were two of them, actually, an older man who did the talking and a youngster along for indoctrination. They brought a satchel of comic-book propaganda with them, then hopped around in my tiny kitchen, shaking off the November chill.

As it happened, the comic books were for sale, and when the pair heard I was a writer, they suggested I buy a copy. "I think you'll appreciate how well it's written," the older man said. In fact, the prose was atrocious. But the message cut through the pedantry like a beam of divine light: Without salvation, there was no way I'd make the best-seller list.

"How about travel guides?" I said.

"Don't hold your breath," said the elder.

The pair showed up several more times that fall, leaving their literature inside the screen door when I wasn't home. But just as I was on the verge of remembering their names, they quit me. Had they known my past, I might not have seemed so hopelessly provincial.

I left college at twenty, and six months later plunged into the spiritual world. Under the wing of a small, nut-brown Indian guru, I meditated daily, chanted phrases in a language I did not understand, and wore loose clothing. Meditation, though it did not change my life, probably did make me easier to live with. But a host of underlying insecurities remained, most of which could be categorized under two subheadings: women and money. With no women and no money in the picture, I soon sought salvation elsewhere.

At the time, I was living in Boulder, Colorado, a town so radiant with new-age idealism that even the mayor wore love beads. Only in Boulder could one have, as I did, an earnest discussion about whether or not I was a real hippie. I was too a hippie, I told a roommate, because I was a vegetarian and didn't believe in war. I was not a hippie, he said, because my hair was too short and I didn't travel around the country in a van. He did. The end.

Boulder packaged spirituality in every conceivable way: in Tarot card readers, in EST seminars, in the Scientology boys and their tin-can E-meters, in tabs of LSD hawked on street corners. Gardeners spoke to invisible fairies in their gardens, and men got in touch with their feminine sides, had a good cry, and found solace in the arms of other men. Almost everyone who was not actually earnest and caring at least tried to act that way, including me. I cut a wide but undistin-

49

guished swath through a half dozen different organizations, trying this, tasting that, a cosmic dilettante. Finally, I ended up in a community whose leader's primary talent, it is clear to me now, was convincing fifty-odd people to pay him a monthly stipend so he could buy a ranch on the Arkansas River, drink Jack Daniel's from the bottle, and diddle every woman he could get his hands on. This last organization was the only one I didn't quit; they booted me out, a decision somberly announced before all at the monthly community meeting. As only those few who have willingly abandoned control of their lives will understand, I was devastated. The next day, I sat under the maple tree in my front yard and accepted consolations from my earnest, caring friends.

But that was the end of it. Afterwards, the occasional seminars I attended held little of interest; I'd heard it all before. Living on tofu and brown rice was getting old. Boulder was not getting old yet, but it would. After seven years of sometimes hard, sometimes not so hard, "inner" work, I had not changed in any essential way. What I essentially remained was this: a twenty-seven-year-old college dropout waiting tables in a Mexican restaurant. Where was Jesus when I needed a real job?

When I moved to Montana three years later I assumed I was through with religion. But it is evidently my karmic destiny to look like a soft touch. For lo and behold, the eternal salvation posse picked up my trail.

Manhattan, Montana, is so small there's only one laundromat in town, and last spring, when it closed for repairs, I was forced to take my wash to the laundromat in the next town east, nine miles distant.

The place was deserted save for one man about my age, who thumbed through a magazine in the corner. I nodded and he nodded back. Then he flipped the magazine shut and dropped it in the rack behind him.

"Y'all from around here?" He was smiling.

I told him I was. More smiles. He was a good-looking guy, muscular and several inches shorter than me. Flannel shirt, jeans.

"I'm here visiting my sister," he said.

"Where from?"

"California now, only I used to live in Georgia."

"So how do you like Montana?"

"It's pretty nice, but I ain't used to this cold rain. I thought it was gonna be a little drier, you know, up here in the mountains and all." He stared at me.

"Not in May," I said. "This is the monsoon season around here."

"You mind if I ask you something?"

Here it came. The smile should have clued me in, but the flannel shirt had caught me off guard—evidently, his wool suit was in the wash.

"Have you been saved?"

As many times as I've been asked that question, it still leaves me groping for words. Saved from what? Extinction? If I say yes, then what? Do I get an award? Do I get money? I could use some money. If I say no, can I get saved during the rinse cycle so I can get back to work? And if I *were* saved, do you think I'd advertise it? Who wants to know, **anyway?** Did God put you up to this? How come you're so short?

"No," I said.

"It ain't that hard."

"That's what they tell me."

"If you want, we could just sit down raht here and pray."

"Pray for what?"

"For what? Why, for your soul, son."

"How old are you?" I said.

"What?"

"How old are you?"

"Thirty-one."

"Well, I'm thirty-four. So see, you can't call me 'son.' I'm three years older than you."

He tapped his fingernail on the lid of a dryer. "Well," he finally said, "it don't really matter."

I shrugged.

"Look," he said, reaching into his billfold. "Here's my card. You want to talk some, you just call. You can even call collect, I'll talk to you." I looked at his card. He was a licensed general contractor. A carpenter, just like Jesus.

I was nearly thirty before I found a life that fit. No earth shaking revelation here—I simply realized, after having tried and failed at nearly everything else the previous twenty-nine years, that my only real talent was writing. I'd have preferred an aptitude for, say, corporate takeovers, but then, I could as easily have found my life's work in a restaurant, gazing into a bus tray of half-eaten tacos. It was touch and go there for awhile.

It was around that time that I left Colorado for Montana, where I'm building a home I have every intention of living in the rest of my life. My friends shake their heads and wonder how this can be. But, despite the cold, there is no place I'd rather live than Montana; despite the poor money, no work I'd rather do than writing. I suppose that means I'm finally satisfied with where I fit into the scheme of things, which is not the same as being happy all the time, something the self-proclaimed healers never told me. Or maybe they did. But with so many talking at once, who was I to listen to?

A few days ago, on an ice-cream run to the convenience store, I spied an unknown, but somehow familiar, pair: two men in pressed suits, one fiftyish, the other a kid barely in his twenties, all knees and elbows. The kid was dripping goodwill. "We went to Yellowstone today," he announced, "and then we went to church and talked about Jay-zuz."

"Uh huh," I said. "Where you two from?"

"Oklahoma."

The older man spoke. "I'm from Churchill originally," he said, mentioning a little community a few miles away. "But that was forty years ago. Lot's changed around here since then. Yellowstone's changed, probably that earthquake they had."

I agreed. Earthquakes certainly do make a mess of things.

"You a carpenter?"

"Sort of," I said. "I'm building myself a house so I dress like this sometimes." I then described my home: extremely well insulated, vapor barrier, energy efficient, etc. Get me going on that subject and I'll talk through a miracle. Throughout, the kid stood two feet from my shoulder and grinned at my ear.

The cashier said that when she'd switched from electricity to natural gas, she'd cut her bill by three-fourths.

Then the kid, his white teeth blazing, said, "Yellowstone is so purty it makes you wonder what heaven is gonna look like."

Pause.

"Well now," I said, "will you look at that." I held up my checkbook for all to see. "No checks. Guess I'll have to come back in a little while for that darned old ice cream." And with that I shot outside. I was halfway to my truck when I heard the door clang open and saw the kid's shadow looming over my shoulder.

Not me, not this time. I broke into a trot, dove in behind the wheel, and goosed it. I caught a glimpse of the kid in the doorway as I left, still smiling, watching me go.

COWBOY POETRY: THESE GUYS ARE SERIOUS

W addie Mitchell wasn't in. You may have seen Mitchell on Johnny Carson—he was written up in *Newsweek* a few years back, then invited to recite cowboy poetry and twirl his handlebar mustache on the show. As I recall, he wore a white hat and sheepskin chaps, the sheepskin chaps notable by their absence on the other guests, including Ed McMahon.

Instead, I spoke with Mitchell's father, in Elko, Nevada. Waddie would be living with them while he got the house he'd just bought in order. But at that particular moment he was out doing a reading, and wouldn't be back until late.

Would he be around in the morning? Mitchell senior just couldn't say. "Pardner," he told me, "that boy is like butter on a hot skillet."

A FAST START

They are leavin' from there but they ain't
*   goin' far*
Or they wouldn't be ridin' as fast as they
*   are.*
For even a fuzzy faced kid ort to know
If you want to go far you must start 'em
*   out slow.*
Or you'll git every thing your hoss has in
*   his hide*
And still be a long ways from the end of
*   your ride*
Jest let him go walkin' along fer a while
A takin' it easy fer over a mile
Then stop. Git your saddle set right on
*   his back.*
And then when you cinch him pull some
*   of the slack.*

Jist hitch up your "Levi's" and fix you a
*   smoke.*
Like a sensible man and a sho'nough cow
*   poke.*
You will soon learn the pace that he
*   travels the best.*
Set down in your saddle and he'll do the
*   rest*
You will find when you're through, if
*   there's any hoss there*
He will last a long time and he'll git you
*   somewhere.*

(Bruce Kiskaddon, sometime
prior to 1924)

All right. I'll admit I've plumb wondered about this stuff.
Most cowboy poetry is right up there with Roy Rogers for
schmaltz. Cowboy poets don't win Pulitzers, nor are they
asked to give readings at presidential inaugurations. Cowboy
poets do not become well paid and undermotivated professors
at universities, which, I hasten to add in deference to several
dedicated and tenured poet friends, is certainly not true of all
academics.

On the other hand, cowboy poetry almost always rhymes,
and it's easy to understand, reassuring to those who, like me,
have wondered over the years why they simply can't fathom
what most contemporary poets are talking about. Is it us or
the words?

Mitchell had been writing poems for close to half the forty-
one years of his life, and reciting them even longer, when he
was approached by Hal Cannon, a Western folklorist from

Great Falls, Montana, with an idea: Cannon and others wanted to put together a one-time cowboy poetry festival in Elko. Mitchell, in a slow, rhythmic lilt, recalled his excitement at the very idea of it: "I guess I was pretty near the only cowboy poet he [Cannon] knew well enough to call. We'd become sort of friends at some different folk festivals where they had folklife arts and crafts. They'd have me come in and not only tell some stories, but braid some rawhide and twist some horsehair, things like that. And he just said, 'Do you think, if we were ever just to get a little weekend poetry festival together, that you'd be interested in helping out?' So I says—I didn't really think anybody'd come—but I said sure, I'd be glad to help him if he did. I thought it'd be a good time getting some of my friends together doing something I loved. I had *no* idea it would ever take off like this."

What cowboy poetry has become, at least for a night or two each year in small towns across the West, is entertainment that rivals movie matinees and rock concerts in popularity. Poets like Mitchell, veterinarian Baxter Black, rancher Wally McRae, and rodeo cowboy Paul Zarzysky are approaching minor celebrity status, and if all the foofaraw is interfering with the chores, well, things could be worse. For the last hundred years or so, no one paid any attention at all.

Cowboy poetry is nothing new. Western newspapers and magazines ran it in the late 1880s, and in 1893, Larry Chittenden's *Ranch Verses* was published. Others followed. *Rhymes from a Roundup Camp* (illustrated by Charles Russell) was released in 1899; *Songs of the Cowboys*, by Howard Jack Thorp, in 1908. Bruce Kiskaddon published *Rhymes of the Ranges* in 1924. Other collections, by various authors, followed in the next two decades. Without fail, they were politely read by the authors' friends, then tossed on a bookshelf, forgotten. "Books never were big sellers," Mitchell says, "but then again, what poetry books are?"

The genre's oral tradition may be what has kept it alive. Mitchell heard recitations first from the cowboys he knew as a boy. "I guess I was twenty-four when I actually started writing poetry seriously, but before that, I had a lifetime tradition of hearing it and reciting it. Not for the public, you know, but for my friends and the other cowboys that I worked with. It's been a tradition that cowboys have done for a long time.

"And I'm convinced that the reason cowboy poetry has gone from generation to generation is due to the fact that it is an oral tradition. When you stop to think about it, you know, the working cowboy spends long periods of time with the same men, and many times in confined situations, even though their work was in the vast openness. Try telling a joke to your friends for about the third time and see what happens. But add a rhyme and a meter to it, and it's like a . . . like a song. People will listen and tend to *want* to listen to it over and over again. Even request it over and over again."

Like most of the best cowboy poets, Mitchell's a captivating storyteller, at home before a crowd, rather surprising for someone who, for most of his life, has been chasing cattle around Nevada. But his ease in front of an audience is natural, not learned. Mitchell chuckled when I asked him if he'd been trained as a speaker. "Oh no, no, I never did any public speaking. I suppose it's just something that didn't ever bother me. I mean, if they had me up in front of people doing Shakespeare I'd probably be nervous as can be. But seeing as how they just want me to do what I do there's never been any problem with that. And the more I do it, the easier it gets."

THE LEGEND OF BOASTFUL BILL

At a roundup on the Gily,
  One sweet mornin' long ago,
Ten of us was throwed right freely
  By a hawse from Idaho.
And we thought he'd go-a-beggin'
  For a man to break his pride
Till, a-hitchin' up one leggin,
  Boastful Bill cut loose and cried—

"I'm a on'ry proposition for to hurt;
I fulfill my earthly mission with a
        quirt;
   I kin ride the highest liver
   'Tween the Gulf and Powder
        River,
And I'll break this thing as easy as I'd
        flirt."

So Bill climbed the Northern Fury
  And they mangled up the air
Till a native of Missouri
  Would have owned his brag was fair.
Though the plunges kep' him reelin'
  And the wind it flapped his shirt,
Loud above the hawse's squealin'
  We could hear our friend assert

"I'm the one to take such rakin's as a
        joke.

61

Some one hand me up the makin's of
    a smoke!
  If you think my fame needs
    bright'nin'
  W'y I'll rope a streak of lightnin'
And I'll cinch 'im up and spur 'im till
    he's broke."

Then one caper of repulsion
  Broke that hawse's back in two.
Cinches snapped in the convulsion;
  Skyward man and saddle flew.
Up he mounted, never laggin',
  While we watched him through our
    tears,
And his last thin bit of braggin'
  Came a-droppin' to our ears.

"If you'd ever watched my habits
    very close
You would know I've broke such rab-
    bits by the gross.
I have kep' my talent hidin'
  I'm too good for earthly ridin'
And I'm off to bust the lightnin's—
    Adios!"

Years have gone since that ascension.
  Boastful Bill ain't never lit,
So we reckon that he's wrenchin'
  Some celestial outlaw's bit.
When the night rain beats our slickers
  And the wind is swift and stout

And the lightnin' flares and flickers,
We kin sometimes hear him shout—

"I'm a bronco-twistin' wonder on the
    fly
I'm the ridin' son-of-thunder of the
    sky.
Hi! you earthlin's, shut your win-
    ders
While we're rippin' clouds to flind-
    ers.
If this blue-eyed darlin' kicks at
    you, you die!"

(Badger Clark)

In 1985, Elko, Nevada, was chosen for the first cowboy poetry gathering. A recent gold-mining boom has changed things, but in January of that year Elko was a one-horse town in the middle of nowhere, stark and cold in the desert winter. Because it was Nevada, slot machines rubbed shoulders with newspaper stands, and because it was Elko, the railroad tracks ran through the middle of town. Through it all, the Humboldt River eased under a white layer of ice, ferrying its load of sand and silt to Rye Patch Reservoir downstream.

The Elko gathering was a long time coming. For several summers, Western folklorists had been tossing around ideas, some project that those from each state could have a hand in. A cowboy poetry gathering was one idea among many, but turned out to be the most versatile, since each state, every-one assumed, had at least a few cowboy poets. The problem was, where?

Hal Cannon, of the Western Folklife Center in Salt Lake

City, was hired to ramrod the search. Cannon soon had several people in a number of different states working on the project, tracking down leads, talking to old-timers at cattle auctions and in cafes. Ultimately, he took a leave of absence from his job to devote full time to the search. Among other efforts, he sent some fifteen hundred letters to western newspaper editors.

The project got off to a crawling start. "It was sometimes very difficult," Cannon said. "I remember being in southern Colorado once at a cattle auction in a cattle arena, asking about cowboy poetry. People looked at me like I was nuts. But there were different ways to approach it. You'd ask some people about the old cowboy songs—everyone thinks of cowboys as having a song tradition—or you'd talk about cowboy storytelling, approach the subject that way. I asked some if they remembered the old western livestock journals, when Bruce Kiskaddon would publish a poem every month. You'd get into the subject a lot of different ways.

"Out of that, we had about fifty or sixty poets that we brought in, and most of them said it would never work to have cowboys reciting and reading their poetry in public, that it was a private tradition. We were as surprised as anyone when it took off. The *cowboys* were as surprised as anyone—surprised that it had such an appeal even to people that were only peripherally involved in ranching. They just didn't realize that it had any value to it at all. But I always saw the power in it, or I wouldn't have quit my job to do it."

Only a couple thousand people attended the first gathering, but the event was an instant hit with the media. CBS and NBC sent reporters, as did major newspapers and magazines from around the country. Poet and humorist Gwen Petersen, of Big Timber, Montana, appeared on the "Tonight Show." Waddie Mitchell made *Newsweek* and the "Tonight Show." Eastern Montana's Wally McRae wrangled an anchor spot on a local television program. Suddenly, cowboy poetry was no longer an obscure tradition practiced by a bunch of guys in lace-up packer boots. It had become an event. Plain old poetry, with verse that rhymed and lyrics that did not sound like they had been written under water, was popular again. Furthermore, cowboy poetry had attracted the one thing that could conceivably make it more all-American than it already was: money. Non-cowboys, including me, would pay to hear the stuff and leave a reading convinced they had got their money's worth.

None of which seems to make much difference to Paul Zarzysky, who began writing poems around the same time he began rodeoing, back in the early seventies, a solid decade before the idea of a cowboy poetry gathering was even conceived. At forty, Zarzysky (rhymes with whisky, he'll tell you) still has the muscular, tapered build of a weight lifter and the thick shoulders of a bull rider, though his favorite event—his only event, in fact—is riding bareback broncs. Zarzysky's stage presence—pure charisma, which his Marlboro man looks have done little to diminish—have made him a real crowd pleaser. But in 1985, the Elko gathering gathered without him. Zarzysky wasn't invited.

"At that point I was writing solely free-verse poems," he says, "and at that first gathering, I think they were looking for people who adhered very strictly to the [rhyming] tradition."

There's no trace of malice in his voice, and one gets the impression he was perfectly happy riding broncs in the summer and bumming odd jobs the rest of the year to make ends meet, willing to wait until the interest in cowboy poetry broadened enough to squeeze in a few noncomformists. It did, and he's been invited to every Elko gathering since 1987. The last few heady years have seen his popularity soar, and he's undoubtedly changed some from the publicity. But not much.

"I didn't even call it cowboy poetry back then," he says, recalling the early days. "I was rodeo'n' hard, and writing poems about those rodeo experiences and emotions, as well as writing poems about every other experience and emotion. I was never a working cowboy, you know. My only contribution to the whole arena of cowboy poetry—I'd rather be called a rodeo poet, in fact—is through rodeo, just the tip of a little finger of what old Teddy Blue Adams was. But rodeo was a major part of my life, and still is."

Zarzysky has been around. He was, for a time, a teacher of technical writing at the University of Montana, which ultimately led to a gig as a creative writing teacher, filling in for Dick Hugo when that renowned Montana poet and professor took sick and died. Zarzysky, a master's degree in creative writing under his platter-sized belt buckle, was felling timber at the time. That's logging to you and me.

"I was working in the woods when they told me Dick had gotten sick. I was up to my elbows in chain-saw parts, but I went over there and talked to the chairman, who asked me if I wanted to fill in for him. I told him, 'Sure, when do you want me to start?' He told me if I ran upstairs maybe I could catch his first class, they were probably still sitting there.

"Later on, I taught a little bit of poetry in the schools, you know, for the Montana Arts Council, but I haven't held a steady job for over six months in my life, and I'm forty years old." Zarzysky chuckled. "I guess I listened to too much Janis Joplin and 'Me and Bobby McGee.' I just wanna be free."

Zarzysky thought about going the college professor route. "The choices were either to go and get a legitimate job, try and start a career in the academic world, or to say piss on it and live out my passions and stay here in Montana. Of course, anyone with a lick of sense would choose the latter, and I did. All I wanted to do was rodeo, ride buckin' horses and write poems. Things haven't changed much twenty years later. That's still about all I want to do."

Now, as it turns out, the demand for performances has given Zarzysky, and a very few other cowboy poets, the opportunity to make rent money and perhaps even eke out a living, however modest that living may prove to be. And Zarzysky, a shade mellower than the burly young logger who took over a college teaching post on the spur of the moment, perhaps even enough of a natural showman to know when to give an audience what it wants, now writes and recites a bit of the more traditional, rhyming poetry as well. In fact, he told me, he sometimes prefers reciting it, finding a timeless magic in the classics of the genre, some written nearly a century ago.

But his heart is still in free verse. "I think the rhyme is a lot tougher to write and write well, and I don't think anyone writes it better than Wallace McRae. He's the best contemporary cowboy poet by miles—by light years ahead of everybody else. But it's not always that way. Rhyme is real tough to write; it's the same old saw you've heard over and over where the rhymes too often dominate: 'the bronc bucked me off, I lost my hat, I'm here to tell you that.' Well, no shit.

"I'm excited by every word in the line. So when I'm doin' the free-verse poems, I'm not preoccupied with making those rhymes. It's like open range, it's before the fences, you know. It's that freedom I really aspire to in everything I do. No rules. Dick Hugo used to say there are no rules. The only rule is, don't be boring."

PARTNER

As you hit ground off Staircase,
number 12, at the state fair
rodeo in Great Falls, it was hard
to hear vertebra cracking
above the murmur of ten thousand
hometown hearts. You
  cowboyed-up
and hid your grimace deep,
walked out of the arena,
stubborn, on sheer pain
and took the ambulance, like a cab,
front seat to Emergency.

Tonight, drunk on Tanqueray,
we vow never again
to mention "broken neck." Instead
we talk tough broncs, big shows
we'll hit down south, and hunting
  ducks
come fall. We straggle home,
moon-struck, to the squawk of
  geese—

a V of snows crisscrossing
and circling the city—screwed-up,
you say, when streetlight glimmer
throws them off plumb.

When my bronc stomped
down the alleyway that night,
I knew down deep our bones and
hearts
were made to break a lot
easier than we'd believe. I felt
your arm go numb in mine,
took the gate, weak-kneed, and
spurred
with only half the try. It's bad
and good some cowboys don't know
tears
from sweat. I folded both
between fringes of your chaps,
packed your riggin' sack neat
as you'd have, and wandered
punch-drunk lost, afraid
into the maze of parking lot.

What's done is done, I know,
but once I killed
at least a dozen singles
in a season, without thinking
how they partner-up for life
and death, how the odd ones
flocking south
survive that first long go alone.
            (Paul Zarzysky, Rough Stock
                Sonnets, Lowell Press*)*

These days, Wally McRae has a foot in two or three different stirrups. Aside from ranching full time near Forsyth, Montana, he's anchoring "The West," a local TV show, acting in summer theater, and, when the mood strikes him, announcing rodeos. But it is his poetry that has made him, if not famous, at least the poet most often associated with the craft, the one nearly everyone else I spoke with mentioned as being one of the best, though he has a thought or two on that subject, which I'll get to presently.

Like almost everyone else, McRae never thought the Elko gathering would fly. There just weren't enough poets around, and who would drive all the way to Nevada to listen to *poetry*, anyway? On top of that, they wanted to make a contest out of the thing: "Mike called me up one day [Mike Corn, a Montana folklorist], and asked me if I knew anything about Elko, Nevada. I said no, but I'd been through there once, back when I was in college. In fact, I'd run out of gas between Elko and Wells. Still didn't remember much about the place, though.

"He said it was kind of a cowboy town. About the right size, they've got a convention center there . . . how would you like to go there and do a cowboy poetry contest? I said, '*contest*?' And he said, 'I don't think that's what we want to do, is it?' And I said, 'Boy, that isn't what *I* want to do.'

"Then he asked me If I'd heard of Capriola's. I said yeah, I'd heard of the Capriola saddle company. And he told me they'd put up a saddle for the winner. So I said, 'Mike, that's not what it's about; it's not about winning. My vote says let's not do it that way.' And it turns out Mike felt that way too. So they didn't have a contest, but they did have a gathering."

When the gathering was over, however, McRae emerged

something of a celebrity, a situation he's not altogether com-
fortable with. "Unfortunately, the gathering *has* become a
contest. And it *has* become about winning and losing. Win-
ning is getting on the Carson show. Winning is having some-
body put me on "The West." Winning is having a videotape
done about you. Winning is having you [me] call and want to
put me in an essay about cowboy poets. But there's losers out
there, too. And that's unfortunate. I think a lot of us, because
of the winning and losing aspect of it, now are writing and
reciting poems for the wrong reasons. But I suppose that's
the nature of the game.

"I just taught a workshop last week in Oklahoma. I was the
only white—there were five instructors, three native Amer-
icans and a black. And we were all complaining about the
popularity, and therefore the dilution and prostitution of that
folk art that we practiced. I said the same thing, too. People
are capitalizing on the popularity of it and violating the craft.
So we talked about it. Is it better to be ignored, and lose that
aspect of your culture? Or is it better for it to be discovered,
and then . . . I don't know. I don't know."

McRae's sincerity has probably doomed him to a life of
second-guessing his own motives. Still, the man is in it for the
long haul; he told me the first poem he recited was at four
years of age. Now he must be pushing sixty, though if he's
not, he looks it. Ranching is a hard go, and all the poetry in
the world won't erase the lines God puts on the face of a
working man.

A few months ago, before this piece was written, I at-
tended a reading given by Gwen Petersen, Zarzysky, and
McRae. Petersen is one of the few women poets around—

71

cowboy poetry being, well, a loose fraternity composed primarily of cowboys, which undoubtedly does not bother Petersen in the least. I've known her casually for several years, and she's nothing if not outspoken. Her poems—she was the first to read that night and had to stand on a box to reach the microphone—lend her a gingham-apron public personae, but cross her and she'll cinch that apron around your neck.

Then came McRae—by turns hilarious and sincere—and finally Zarzysky, who strode away from the podium, leaned out over the very edge of the stage, and with his thumbs hooked in his belt and his Tom Waits voice, told of the smell and the sound of rodeo; of the horses and the piss and the mud and the miles of it. Their poems, not all of them maybe, but some of them, stayed with me through the night and into the next day. But now there's just this one, a show-closing McRae composition that he called like a square dance, tapping his foot in 4/4 time. Take it from here, Wally, because you're a lot better at this than I am.

Put That Back . . . Hoedown

Supercolliders, M H D,
  and coal-fired powerplants.
The fiddles croon; sweet is the tune.
  Now everybody dance.
For it's jobs, growth and money,
  and a song the band can play;
We'll revel through the midnight hours
  until the break of day.
Now balance with your partner
  and the gal across the hall,

For Alamand's left the cowboy life
  and he's gonna have a ball.
Promenade all to the Union Hall.
  Get hand-stamped there for life.
Sashay out with benefits for you,
  your kids and wife.
Right hand across to the MX pad.
  Tell Ivan, "Howdy-do."
Left hand back with lead gloves on
  and "General, how are you?"
Shimmy down in a Texas Star,
  with a chain saw in your hand,
And clear-cut tress two centuries old
  to McCulloch's Ragtime Band.
Hum, hum uranium.
  Oh hear them Geigers rattle.
This beats to hell, any-old-day,
  them days with longhorn cattle.
Buy a modern box lunch. Pay a bunch
  for a Hostess Twinkie, pard.
Promenade with Gatorade
  and puke out in the yard.
Now, do-si-do a Case backhoe
  for another septic tank
And two-step to your Harley too
  and climb a spoil bank.
Put yer little foot down. Don't be slow.
  Hear them hydraulics whine.
Another day. The pay ain't hay
  in the mother-lovin' mine.
Them power lines hum at all times
  from here down to L.A.
Turkey in the straw. Change that law
  to make them hummers pay.

73

Pay the gent thirty percent.
*   Too much? We'll cut her down*
To an itty bitty pittance,
*   or they'll close down my hometown.*
Town and country get along,
*   or we'll condemn your ranch.*
'Cause meat it comes from IGA.
*   Now everybody dance.*
Dance around the outside.
*   Boil that cabbage down.*
Wheat and cows and sheep don't pay?
*   Then ship yer kids to town.*
We'll pay them dough, boy, dough, boy, dough.
*   And you can sell the farm.*
Or put it in the CRP
*   It won't do any harm.*
Harm onee is good for me and you
*   and her and him.*
Chicken in the bread pan
*   pickin'out dough and palladium,*
Platinum and chromate ore.
*   Watch out . . . Another truck!*
Lucky thing we come yer way.
*   Oh, Lucky Lady Luck!*
Oh! Looky here the old coon dog
*   has done laid down and died.*
They're mining copper once again
*   across that big divide.*
Divide and conquer. Left and right,
*   split right down the middle.*
Cotton-eyed Joe and do-si-do.
*   Now let's hear that fiddle.*
Fiddle again with big BN
*   and they won't haul yer grain.*

Massa's on the cold cold ground.
  I'm bucked off in the rain.
Reinin' left, Reinin' right,
  on my reinin' hoss;
Hired hand up and quit today.
  Now who'll be my boss?
Circle two-step. Circle wagons
  Who's the Circle jerk?
Minors packin' fake I.D.'s
  Miners out of work.
Workin' on the railroad
  all the live-long day.
Skin the Cat. Dog the steer.
  Take Chapter Twelve today.
It's polka dot in the old oil spot
  as we poke that drill bit down.
Varsouvian on the old hardpan;
  then hoedown down downtown.
Chicken Reel'n' how ya feel
  as we rip across The West?
Turkey Trot in the new mall lot
  with the gal you love the best.
Let's all join hands and Circle West,
  and let the moon shine in.
Let down yer hair and rip and tear,
  destruction ain't no sin.
Now Home Sweet Home to the mobyle home,
  (a 'sixty-nine New Moon).
Crank up the Ford. Don't be bored,
  just hum a cowboy tune.
Thank the boys with 'lectric toys
  that played the country dance.
Though there's damn little Country left,
  pay your money, take yer chance.

The country Dance ain't got no chance
  if Mother Earth's a whore.
Heel and toe and away we go.
  Goin' . . . Gone.
There ain't no more.
        (*Wally McRae,* Things of Intrinsic Worth,
                            Outlaw Books)

LIZARD
HEAVEN

> The desert will still be here in the spring.
> And then comes another thought. When I
> return will it be the same? Will I be the
> same? Will anything ever be quite the
> same again? If I return
> —Ed Abbey, Desert Solitaire

Around the waist-high concrete wall of the Desert View observation platform are bolted a half dozen brown plywood boxes. Each encloses a sloping pane of black plexiglass, and sawed-in portholes topside provide views of the Grand Canyon, which snakes into the hazy distance a mile below. But something's wrong. The canyon, reflected on these obsidian plates, is upside down.

Within the boxes we spy our destination. The granite escarpment of the Little Colorado River dangles above an azure landscape; clouds flit about like bleached tumbleweeds. Doug and I simply can't figure these boxes out. What will those Arizona guys think of next?

Later that night, while we eat the world's worst pizza in Tusayan, an earthquake rattles the silverware. We agree: better an earthquake than the pizza.

Doug Smith and I have been friends since our high school football days. In college, when we were freshman roommates at Colorado State, he was fat, but no longer. Among his other diversions, he now races his bicycle through the streets of Seattle for two hours daily and trots up Mt. Rainier on weekends. He's built like a wrestler and can hike forever. For that matter, so can I.

No I can't. Like Doug, my left knee was overhauled years

ago. Unlike Doug, whose legs were equipped at birth with leaf-spring quadriceps, downhill hikes give me fits. And it is one hell of a long downhill hike to the bottom of the Grand Canyon. By the time we weave through the pinyon-juniper woodlands on the rim, through the yucca plants and barrel cactus and sandstone below Cardenas Butte, and finally across the sun-blasted shale to the river, it has been six black hours. Five thousand feet above us, last week's snows blush rose with the evening.

For this week-long backpacking trip, I carried only the essentials: a stove, a sleeping bag and foam pad, and a copy of Ed Abbey's *Desert Solitare*. Doug supplied food; the meals were precooked at his home and dehydrated in an electric food dryer. We had matches, white gas, rain gear, down vests, and sunscreen; first-aid kits, wool socks, and capilene underwear. My blue capilene long johns jutted from beneath my hiking shorts; in my canvas fedora and expensive boots, I bore a horrifying resemblance to a rugged yuppie on maneuvers.

After filling our canteens with the Colorado's turquoise water, we discussed strategy. A day earlier, our original plan had been scrapped when we discovered, too late, that the road to the trail head we'd chosen traversed twenty-four miles of axle-deep gumbo. A circuitous and snowy thirty-hour drive from Montana had nearly ended right there, before we'd set foot in the canyon. At the back-country office in South Rim Village we'd huddled over maps, studying alternative routes, but nearly every one had been reserved months earlier.

A man who overheard our plight suggested we hike to the

Little Colorado River. The park ranger, who had been forced to refuse all our alternative requests, brightened with relief. "That's one of my favorite trips," he said, "and we may have an opening." The stranger nodded. "A real pretty hike. And there's never anyone else up there." When the ranger told us the route was open, we scrambled to sign the registration form.

Now, with the months of planning behind us, we were inside at last. The canyon of the Little Colorado was thataway, a two-day walk upstream. Doug squinted at a bank of wafer-like clouds to the west, then up at the sun, then back at the clouds again. "Rain before tomorrow, guaranteed," he said.

Rain would have been fine with me. In Arizona as elsewhere, the '88 drought had scorched the earth, and anything not within feet of the river was dead or heading in that direction. No water flowed in the side canyons; what greenery there was lay in state beneath a shroud of red dust.

Yet that night was far colder than either of us had anticipated, and we shivered in our bags while the river fretted twenty feet away. I pulled on my polypro underwear and finally a down vest and an extra pair of socks.

Shortly after sunrise, the temperature rocketed to seventy degrees. After checking my boots for scorpions, I walked to the river and discovered to my dismay that it had risen a foot overnight and now flowed milky brown. Behind me, Doug was bemoaning his lack of a water filter, an item his twin brother had volunteered prior to our trip. "Maybe the river will drop back down again," I said. Doug, who is nobody's fool, gave me a withering stare. Evidently, the snow on the rim was melting. Our trip had coincided with the unfortunate first stage of runoff: The same warm weather that would make for pleasant hiking would also, via melting snow, churn the river into undrinkable brown ooze.

Back in camp, we discovered more good news: Pack rats had commandeered our groceries. A nickle-sized hole in the food bag spewed an incriminating trail of filberts and peanut m&m's; looked like the little bastards went straight for the trail mix. No telling what kind of diseases they carried, but we'd eat what they left or go hungry.

Our destination that morning was the Palisades Creek drainage, a four-mile hike upstream. With luck, we'd make camp by early afternoon and have the remainder of the day to rest and cook. To my vast relief, this was the shortest leg of the trip. My knee still ached, despite painkillers and a long soak in the river the previous afternoon.

In addition, the hike in had left both of us with contracting calf muscles, and for the first quarter mile we tottered along as though on high heels, legs frozen in living rigor mortis. The uphills were the worst. Even with a forty-five-pound pack, my ankles refused to flex under the load, and my shins and thighs burned in protest. But the ensuing miles hammered out the knots, and soon we picked up the pace, Doug rocking from side to side in a mile-eating, bowlegged glide, while I brought up the rear.

The slope of this section of the Tonto Platform was studded with what appeared to be volcanic outcroppings, pumice-like stone as abrasive to the touch as a sharp cheese grater. Doug told me that he had once climbed a wall of similar rock, fallen, and though roped in, had careened back and forth across a dozen feet of sheer cliff, leaving his face looking as though it had been shaped with a wood rasp. I vowed once again to avoid rock climbing, an easy vow to keep since the sport terrifies me.

Higher up we found Utah agave, their dead stalks towering above us, amid scattered clumps of barrel cactus. As a youngster, I'd watched a TV episode of "High Chaparral" in which Blue, the son of a wealthy Arizona rancher, had saved the life of his dehydrated father by hacking the top off a colossal barrel cactus and stuffing the plant's wet pulp in his father's mouth. Sounded plausible then, but I've since learned it doesn't work that way. Barrel cactus render more pulp than water, and knifing cactus plants is frowned upon by the Park Service.

Then we were dropping again. Below the agave and barrel cactus, down through the gray volcanic stone, and finally to the sandbar itself, to the river, to the willows up ahead. Palisades Creek: A canyon wren's descending notes fall as though drawn to the water.

All we could see of the Grand Canyon were the walls that loomed eternally above us, blacking out the river after four every afternoon. That's the problem with being inside; you don't see as much of the canyon as you would if you'd stayed on the rim with the Japanese tourists and their Nikons.

Doug was down by the river. He'd found a ponderous three-foot wedge of sandstone he planned to use as a backrest, and as I watched from flat on my back in the sand, he

83

tilted the slab on edge, flopped it over, tilted it up again, and flopped it over, approaching me thus for fifty yards and a full ten minutes. Doug's energy amazes everyone. Out of college, with a forestry degree, he landed a job with the Oregon branch of the BLM, where, armed with a can of orange spray paint and marking ribbons, he plotted logging tracts. One day, sick of tromping the same wet woods, he painted a tree orange from the ground up and flagged every branch on it. Shortly afterwards he quit, got a master's degree in forest economics, and landed a position with a private utility in Seattle, a well-paying job that suited him intellectually but left little time for backpacking and climbing, the sports he loves. Three years of sixty-hour weeks was enough of that, and he took a cut in pay to take a job with the Forest Service, where he's an economic planner, with free time to spare.

Doug's backrest was in place now, propped up with a plank he'd scavenged from beneath the leafless bushes surrounding our camp. A lizard, emerald throat pulsing, scampered to the top of the slab, then bobbed up and down in a series of methodical push-ups. Life is no cakewalk for these tiniest of the Grand Canyon's dinosaurs. Among hundreds of similar lizards we'd seen was one minus a tail; another, hollow as an Easter egg, had a hole pecked through the parchment skin stretched over its ribs.

While Doug cooked dinner (spaghetti tonight), I scrubbed my socks in the river and draped them on a willow sapling. Back in camp, I fiddled with the pumps and valves on my stove, lit a match, and instantly ignited a square yard of dry grass. I stared aghast as the fire raced toward the brush behind us, then slapped the stove toward the river. Doug and I furiously smothered the blaze with sand.

"Christ," I said.

"Maybe you don't have to pump it that hard."

"I guess not."

Doug sifted through his pack for a vial of seasonings, while I gazed at the still ticking stove, then up, at a wedge of blue and unclouded sky.

"Doug?"

"What?"

"Rain before tomorrow, guaranteed."

Doug gave me the finger.

By dinner I'd read half of *Desert Solitaire*. In the late fifties, Abbey was a park ranger in Arches National Monument, not far from here. He railed against paved roads, tourists, picnic tables, and the National Park Service, and his caustic voice was heard and applauded around the country. Yet one by one, his canyons and deserts disappeared. Before Glen Canyon sank beneath the waters of Lake Powell, Abbey and a friend, Ralph Newcomb, floated through, and an entire chapter describes their trip. Read the book; you and I will never see the place. The Bureau of Reclamation beavers destroyed it as surely as Moses and the Red Sea destroyed the Philistines, and with very nearly the same omniscient wave of a hand. But then, why should I care? It wasn't *my* canyon.

Maybe it was the lousy water that night, or Abbey's bittersweet prose, but after dark the conversation drifted across space. The cliffs to the east and west blacked out all but a narrow band of stars, and with the moon away from that place—we never did see it—each pinprick of light stood apart from its neighbors, explicit and sovereign. We talked.

"The thing is," Doug said as he handed me a cup of coffee, "everyone who's seen aliens says the same thing."

"What's that?"

"They get beamed into spaceships and *probed*."

I agreed that aliens were a real problem.

"Look," Doug said, "I'm just telling you what I saw on TV. Once they were up in the spaceships they were probed, then beamed back to earth, where they forgot most of it. Brainwashed, I suppose."

"How were they probed?"

"I don't know, with thermometers. They were laid out like pet gerbils and then probed. And everyone who's seen them describes them the same way. The drawings and police sketches all match."

"Makes you wonder."

"Yes."

Doug's stove sputtered out, and I pitched the rest of my coffee into the sand. I hunched into my sleeping bag, zipping the hood around my ears, then wedged my butt into the hollow beneath my foam pad. The river purred and faded.

Next I was downfield, Doug's man in a heap on the line of scrimmage, high school ball. The pigskin is up and floating, black discs hovering overhead. Aliens. I twist my bag toward Doug, but it's Abbey's gaunt face I see, laughing his fool head off.

When the sun cleared the canyon walls it was instantly hot. My socks still hung from the willow shoot, and the sand around them was filigreed with lizard tracks. No telling what they thought about this.

We had a four- or five-mile hike ahead of us to the Little Colorado, and we flirted with the idea of hiking up and back in one day. Thank God we decided not to. Once past the sand-bar, the trail shot uphill, and my legs, still aching, quivered with the exertion.

The trail climbed steadily, meandering through side can-yons en route, and we soon realized that our Park Service map was scaled much too large to depict the dozens of smaller side canyons we had traversed. By noon we had hiked at least five miles, but the Little Colorado, which we had hoped to reach by then, was still beyond us, perhaps another three or four miles. Worse, it was the hottest day so far. The rock under our feet blurred as we trudged ahead, swaddled in a cocoon of heat and dust.

Eventually, the trail leveled off, but as we approached a two-hundred-yard stretch that clung to the very edge of a sheer, six-hundred-foot cliff, Doug had a sobering thought: What if there was another earthquake while we were out there?

It was possible. When tremors had shaken the pizza parlor two days before, Doug and I had gawked at a wagon-wheel chandelier swinging over our heads, but the parlor's atten-dants had seemed reassuringly bored. Yet later that night there had been another quake, more violent than the first.

But of course it wouldn't do to turn back now. Beyond the precipice, the sandstone walls flanking the Little Colorado had curved into view, at most another two miles up the trail. With a measured stride, Doug walked ahead, and when he gained the other side he paused while I snapped his picture. My turn. For Chrissake don't look down.

My next memory is of the last few yards of ledge and Doug's broad grin. I grinned back, and soon we were howling with laughter and flinging boulders into the chasm behind us.

The Little Colorado snakes southeast through the Navajo Indian Reservation, an utterly barren landscape whose handsome residents hawk turquoise watchbands from greasewood lean-tos bordering Highway 89. Here on the extreme western edge of the park, we were just a few miles from the reservation, and its effects were obvious the moment the first threads of the Little Colorado wove into view: The river was brown and sullen with eroded soil.

This was a wrenching shock; it was the Little Colorado, not runoff, that had been polluting our drinking water. Less than a hundred yards upstream, above the confluence of the two rivers, sparkled the clear flows of the main Colorado, as alluring as Odysseus's sirens and just as inviolate: There was simply no way we could get over there. Up close, the waters of the Little Colorado were far worse than we had imagined. The stuff looked like drilling mud and slithered, rather than flowed, over the rocks in midstream. After Doug and I inventoried our last quart of "clean" water, the truth hit us like a forearm smash from a saguaro cactus: This was what we'd be drinking tonight. But only tonight. We unanimously abandoned plans of staying longer than one night, since the idea of drinking a drop of that water more than necessary was abhorrent to both of us. That evening, a billowing front scudded over the rim, and the willows along the Little Colorado rattled like chopsticks. But by midnight the stars were out, and we slept fitfully until dawn.

When next the sun blazed down, we were beyond the precipice we'd crossed the day before and marching steadily toward the Palisades Creek drainage. Once we hit the river, we dumped the contents of our canteens and filled them with the comparatively clean water of the main Colorado. But our diet of mineral-laced river mud was telling; Doug claimed he'd trade a year's worth of mimeographed Christmas form letters for one beer and a water purifier. At *least* a year's worth.

Upon reaching Palisades Creek, we had a brief discussion. If we decided to continue beyond our first night's camp and up the next trail out, we'd have three more days to kill. As it stood, we were low on fuel and equally low on ambition. A cold beer *did* sound good. And although we'd taken pains to purify the water, it was obvious to both of us that the essential filth of the stuff would catch up with us sooner or later. On the other hand, we'd driven over a thousand miles through a blizzard to hike in the Grand Canyon, and neither one of us wanted to be the first to admit he'd had enough.

"There was water in all the side canyons last time I was here," Doug said, brushing sand from his bare knees.

"Me too. And I'm not sure I'm up to another ten-mile hike in this heat." I leaned my pack against the sandstone backrest, which Doug had reassembled upon our return. He hung his cap from a blackened tamarisk limb, his transparent blond hair glistening with sweat.

Doug spoke again. "I don't mind the hike," he said, "but this water is killing me. That's what's fun about the Grand Canyon this time of year, the water in the side canyons."

"How much gas do you have left?"

"Not much."

"We could get another pizza in Tusayan."

"Shit."

Dinner was vegetarian stew. Doug's meals were better than expected, but a bit on the skimpy side. Doug had not forgotten his roly-poly days and strictly regulates his diet. But counting calories was the last thing I was interested in on this camping trip, and I was constantly rummaging through the food bags for snacks, dreaming of Hershey bars and peanut butter.

I'd set up my stove in the midst of the charred moonscape I'd created two nights before. In the days following that incident, I'd ironed out the stove's operational difficulties, but now I couldn't find my spoon, which I'd been using to measure coffee. I was sure it had been there a moment ago.

"Doug, did you take my spoon?"

"No."

"You didn't borrow it for just a second?"

"No."

A quick search of my pack did not turn up the spoon. "I think the pack rats took my spoon," I said.

"Why would they do that?"

"They like shiny things."

"Oh."

"So I'm going to look for it," I said.

"All right."

I stood up and looked for my spoon, but no spoon. "I guess I'll have to carve one," I said.

As I searched the sandbar for a suitable piece of driftwood, Doug waved. He'd found my spoon, stashed with our plastic scrubby in the bushes behind camp.

"They really did take your spoon," he said. This seemed to amaze him.

"You thought I was lying?"

"Of course."

Much to my delight, Doug produced an additional package of spaghetti and agreed to cook it while I read *Desert Solitaire*. But before I could open the book, Doug yelped and pointed at the river. "Rafters!" he said. Instantly he was up and sprinting. "Beer! Beer!" he screamed. The rafts' occupants, out of earshot in midriver, waved pleasantly.

"Beer!" Doug shrieked again. He pointed frantically at his mouth.

For five minutes the silver crafts drifted by, each oared by a man, each with a bikini-clad woman propped on the bow. When the last raft bobbed away downstream, Doug turned his back to the river. "You'd think they could part with one lousy beer," he said.

And so we planned to leave a day early. But that night, before we slept, a directive was furrowed in the hot sand of the riverbank, in letters visible from midriver: FUCK THE COMMMIE RAFTERS. Would Abbey have been as eloquent?

Our final evening's campsite was crowded with backpackers—college students, evidently; they bantered and flitted

91

about like chickadees. Up and down the river people stooped to wash dishes and fill canteens. Since we were nearly out of gas—literally and figuratively—and would also run out of food before the evening was over, this would be our last night in.

To make absolutely sure we ran out of food, Doug cooked everything we had left. That night's entrees were spaghetti and moosewood stew *and* beef Stroganoff. We were finishing up the stew when a woman, older than the college girls we'd been watching, walked into camp and squatted on a boulder near Doug. From where I sat I had a clear shot of her knees, prickly with blond stubble. No earth mother this; she'd shaved her legs.

She had hiked down by herself and planned to camp for several days before hiking out again. She told us that it wasn't the first time she'd been to the Grand Canyon, and we soon learned that she'd hiked throughout the Southwest. Apparently, canyon hiking was her thing, and she did enough of it that we both wondered how she found time to make a living. She explained: "I just hang out. You know."

Coke dealer.

Unfortunately, she wasn't hungry, so while she talked we cleaned out our food bags, indelicately stuffing ourselves beyond propriety. The year before, she told us, she'd been backpacking in the Escalante, a drainage of the Colorado River.

"I've been there myself," I said.

"When?"

"Fifteen years ago."

"Well, it's changed. They're planning to put a road through."

I was in high school then. The Escalante was a slit in the desert, a descent into a world of soaring sandstone arches and clear-stream side canyons. Wading up the six-inch-deep Escalante River one day, I'd found a hen rainbow, all those miles up from Lake Powell to spawn. I had reached down and cradled her in my hands, then gently returned her to the water. Nearly dead from exhaustion, she had made no effort to escape. Now a road would be put in, and the canyon would become a tour loop for Winnebagos. Abbey wrote of the place:

> *Walking up the Escalante is like penetrating a surrealist corridor in a Tamayo dream: all is curved and rounded, the course of the mainstream and canyon as indirect as a sidewinder, winding upon itself like the intestines of a giant.*

Substitute "driving" for "walking" and you can flush the rest of that remarkable prose right down the toilet. After Glen Canyon, you'd think they would have learned.

When she left it was nearly dark. A squadron of bats lanced through the insects buzzing overhead, insects that had not been there a week before. Beside me, a lady bug traversed the length of a willow sapling, laboriously detouring the new buds splitting its red bark. Of course. It was spring!

By six thirty the next morning we had gained the Tonto Platform and paused to rest. At this early hour the russet and ocher of the canyon walls were dim pastels as yet unilluminated by the sun, which roared silently below a bulging pink

93

line on the north rim. This was the view that had escaped us for five days on the river, the view we had come for.

Within days of my return to Montana, Ed Abbey would be dead, and I'd deal with the death of a man I would never know in my own way. But now, for the next few minutes, all I wanted to do was look.

WHY BEER IS BETTER THAN ICE FISHING

(In which our hero finds something else to do)

It's pretty darn cold up here in January, a fact the newest wave of immigrants, post-California neo-cowboys, probably didn't reckon on when they bought their ten-acre ranchettes in the Gallatin Valley. Not that they stick around when the snow flies. But enough character assassination.

Among the few places Californians do not yet own are the prairie flats above Canyon Ferry Reservoir, where vacant twenty-acre parcels have been for sale for at least the half dozen years I've been here, and probably will be forever. Barren, dusty, and utterly level, the lots command a view of a herd of antelope and a handful of tract homes on the edge of Townsend, including a hot-pink number owned by one of the protagonists of this story. Beyond, the reservoir maunders into the blue distance, clusters of ice fishermen tilting into the gales that howl down the Elkhorns and across one of the state's largest continuous ice cubes.

Ice fishing is active sport only to those same feeble souls contemplating a winter of serious television or indoor golf. Canyon Ferry is big with trout fishermen in the summer, but it's the perch that keep the place hopping from December on. This despite the fact that they're found under an eighteen-inch lid of ice, way down there in their silent, amniotic world, living out desperate lives. No one cares where the perch go after the thaw. They're seen only in the glaring light of January afternoons, drumming out their existence on the hard pack.

A few years back, novelist Jim Harrison wrote a piece entitled "Ice Fishing, The Moronic Sport," which has evolved into something of an underground classic among we morons who actually read articles other than those published in the

97

hook and bullet magazines, many dozens of which are penned by me, in case you were wondering.

In the shantytowns that spring up on Lake Michigan, Harrison found men peering through holes in the floors of blacked-out fishing shacks, swaddled in yards of wool, drinking. Like the Michigan boys, we ice fishermen crave beer, and the cheaper the better.

Since I've been drinking cheap beer since high school, I slid into ice fishing with only minor adjustments for fit. My friend Paul Updike, who lives in the aforementioned hot-pink house on the edge of Townsend, phoned with an invitation, so early one morning I loaded my truck with what little gear I owned at the time and headed north to Canyon Ferry.

Updike is a sometime fishing guide to Ted Turner, a part-time realtor, and a former Vietnam combat photographer, who, for reasons I suspect are due to ongoing shell shock, is convinced that fishing is best half an hour before and half an hour after dawn, absolutely the coldest sixty minutes of any day, period. As it turned out, he wasn't the only one who felt that way. As we pulled into the parking lot overlooking the lake, lanterns blazed at us from the miles of ice below. Two of them. Evidently, we'd beat the crowds.

Hard-core fishermen buy motorized augers, which will drill through two feet of basaltic reservoir ice in less time than it takes to tell about it. This can be a real advantage when the fish are moving, but the torque on these rotary monsters—some nearly as tall as Paul himself—is frightful, so Updike saves wear and tear on his bad back by using a hatchet instead. The trick is to find holes abandoned a day earlier. The ice isn't as thick there as elsewhere, he explained, and holes

98

can quickly be reopened. Updike and I trooped around, shivering, until he found a spot pitted with six-inch craters, a spot that looked exactly like the half dozen other places we'd already passed. But this was it; we were right across from such and such a point, where everyone was killing them the day before yesterday. He pointed into the blackness. I couldn't help but observe that everyone sure didn't seem to be flocking to the point this morning. Updike suggested I screw myself. I hopped from foot to foot, my hands in my pockets, watching him chop. Occasionally I scooped the slush out of the holes with a metal ladle, then stood in the slush to see if my new boots would freeze to the ice. They would.

For awhile, Canyon Ferry had been big news. Perch fishermen came from all over the state when the schools were moving, and men (and a very few women) in red or orange parkas, kids on skates, and the odd painted shanty lent a festival air to an otherwise dismally bleak landscape. Eventually, someone in Townsend, a pleasant little town of fifteen hundred, which, like every other pleasant little town in Montana, is perennially strapped for cash, hit on the idea of a perch fishing derby. The night before the actual derby, there would be a dance, a Calcutta auction, and cut-rate drinks in local bars. Advertisements were circulated in newspapers. A mention of the event in a report I wrote for *Field & Stream* was posted in half the stores in town. By all accounts, the derby was a great success, undoubtedly because all but two or three hours of the activities took place in bars rather than out on the ice. Even the perch cooperated. The winning team caught two five-gallon *buckets* of the little fish.

When Updike had opened several holes, we loaded his

weapons: two-foot rods baited with comatose maggots. Maggots must be kept from freezing, so you keep a vial containing several dozen of the little creatures packed in sawdust in your shirt pocket, next to your breast and close to your heart. Stashed in the refrigerator between trips, they'll last all season. Not the most appetizing sight alongside the leftover chateaubriand, perhaps, but it isn't like you just threw them in there to fend for themselves.

Perch hover in schools just above the bottom, in anything from two to a hundred feet of water. Paul and I baited hooks, dropped lines in holes, then sprang back to watch, lest the rods be wrenched from our hands. As it happened, the sum total of our activity for the next two hours consisted of just that: watching. Now and then Updike would nudge a rod tip with his boot. "Gets their attention down there," he said.

"Sure is good we got here early," I said.

Then, one of the rods twitched and plunged tip first into a hole. Updike scampered out and hauled up line hand over hand, disengaged a thrashing ten-inch perch, and threw the line back down the hole. Almost immediately another rod arced down, then another. For twenty minutes the two of us hauled fish out of the ice as fast as we could crawl or slide from one hole to the next, giggling like twelve-year-olds. When the school finally passed and the action abruptly stopped, we were surrounded by dozens of bent and semifrozen little yellow fish, like so many Chee-tos flung across the ice. Updike scooped them up one by one and tossed them in a bucket. "Can't fillet them when they're frozen solid," he said.

*   *   *

100

By the end of that first season, I'd bought six new ice rods of my own, a Swedish ice auger, jigs, spinners, and all kinds of other interesting junk, including a red plastic sled to haul the stuff around on. I found a pair of used wool pants in an army surplus store and relocated a pair of down mittens I hadn't worn in years. I bought a cooler for my beer and maggots and binoculars for reconnaissance. When Updike phoned again I didn't need much persuasion to agree to a trip the next day. At four thirty the following morning, I loaded my gear in the back of my truck, deciding, on the spur of the moment, to take my idiot-savant springer spaniel, Poke, along as well. I didn't learn until five thirty that Updike had unilaterally re-arranged our game plan. We'd be picking up a woman who'd mentioned at some undetermined point the previous week that she wouldn't mind going ice fishing herself one of these days, it'd been awhile since she'd been out. Too busy modeling lingerie in Helena.

"Are you sure she wants to go with *us*?" I gazed at my wool pants, unwashed these many months. Ice fishing is hardly the rage among any of the women I know, and most have never heard of such a thing. Those that have consider the sport a sort of retrograde pastime for the chronically unemployed.

Updike rolled his eyes. "You won't believe this chick," he said. His teeth sparkled from behind his red beard. Updike is built like a leprechaun and is forever peering skyward. He made curves with his hands. "She's built like a *Playboy* fold-out, Carty. No shit."

"She said to pick her up? This morning? It's not even six."

He shrugged. "That's what she said," he said.

101

"She's got a boyfriend."

"Of course she's got a boyfriend. In this town she could have thirty-eight and a half of them. If she didn't have a boyfriend, there'd be something wrong with her. And there's nothing wrong with her. N.O.T.H.I.N.G. So believe me, she's got a boyfriend."

"And then what?"

"What do you mean, 'and then what?' "

"I mean, what are we going to do with her? What if she gets cold? I don't want to have to bait her hook."

Updike placed his arched fingertips against the frost on his living-room window, as if trapping a cup. "I'm a photographer. I'm gonna shoot some pictures. And besides that, you're going to thank me for this."

"So am I a photographer." I was feeling a bit churlish after all. What did I care who he'd invited? I'd brought my dog.

A few minutes later Paul knocked gently on the door of a trailer house. I stood behind him, peering through a fog of breath. The floor of the porch bounced, and the door creaked open.

"Oh, Paul. It's you. Geez, you scared me."

"Hi, Lucy. This is my friend Dave. You ready to go?" Lucy had thrown a bathrobe on and hugged it across her chest. A velour belt dangled from one side and curled around her ankle. She shook her head and smiled.

"I guess I sort of forgot you were coming. I haven't got any of my stuff together." A loop of brown hair slid across her nose and she tugged it out of the way. "Maybe you could just go on ahead. I'll get out there when I wake up. I think all my stuff is in Ron's truck anyway."

Back in my Toyota, I sipped on a cup of coffee. "Bet she was up all last night thinking about this trip," I said. We were crawling toward the reservoir on a rutted two-track, easing over the shale under my balding retreads. "Bet she just couldn't wait."

"I'm not kidding," Updike said. "She really likes to fish."

"Uh huh. So who else have you got lined up for us today?" Poke whined from the back.

"Well, I sort of invited this sports reporter from channel four, but I don't know if she's coming or not. It would be good publicity for the derby, though."

"You're kidding."

"No. She's a real nice gal. About twenty-eight. You've probably seen her on TV."

"I haven't got a TV."

"Whatever."

I eased the truck to a stop on an overlook and hopped out the door. The temperature had plunged since dawn, and the sun shone bitterly bright. No wind, no sound other than the distant muffled boom of cracking ice. I opened the door on the topper and Poke shot out into an immediate squat. A wisp of acrid steam curled straight up.

"Jesus, it's cold out here," Updike said. He rocked back and forth on the front seat, trying to pull his thick coveralls over a pair of insulated boots. I loaded our gear on my sled and trudged toward the reservoir. Paul caught up with me shortly. We had a walk ahead of us.

Most of the locals routinely drive their vehicles across the lake, and the two feet of ice under our feet would probably support a fleet of 747s. But I have visions of a bubbling de-

103

scent to the bottom of the reservoir, my truck a sort of inverted aquarium through which curious throngs of perch stare while I claw at the windows. Not long ago, a pickup on this same lake careered into an open lead and sank like a rock in fifteen feet of water. The driver and passenger bailed out at the last minute and lived to pay a crew of scuba divers to haul the truck out again. But one of the divers, in a freak accident, drowned during the attempt. I watched them winch the truck out the next week, water pouring out the windows as though from a resurrected galleon. Forever since, in the few times I have stupidly allowed myself to be talked into riding in a car on lake ice, I have ridden with one hand clutching the door handle and a prayer in my heart. So it was with some apprehension that I watched a white Oldsmobile rumble toward us an hour later, ice booming under its tires. It was the reporter.

After introductions, Updike mentioned that we were expecting another gal along any minute, who would be much more photogenic than either of us. I shot him a glance. She nodded, said she'd walk around and film a little if that was okay. She was quite pleasant, so I volunteered Poke as a model, getting him to hold one of the frozen perch we'd caught while she shoved a camera in his face. Poke, who lives for that kind of attention, thumped his tail on the ice. Updike and I had not yet connected with a school, but there were enough fish running to keep us milling around the rods, despite the cold. I wrapped my parka hood around my face and pulled a scarf over my nose.

By and by, a truck approached, skidding to a stop behind the Oldsmobile. An apparition in a bright red parka hopped out. Lo and behold, it was Lucy the lingerie lady. She smiled at all of us and began sliding buckets of rods over the tailgate.

I walked over to lend a hand. "This stuff all yours?"

"Not all of it," she said. She lit a tremendously elegant cigarette. "Some of it belongs to a friend. We went halves on the auger."

"I'm Dave," I said. "I guess Paul isn't going to introduce us."

"Oh, that's right. You were there this morning. I was sort of sleepy, I guess. I'm Lucy." She extended a mittened hand.

"Yeah. Sorry about all that. Paul thought you'd be up."

"Well, you know Paul." She smiled in his direction. Updike grinned back. Everyone was smiling and grinning, delighted to be freezing to death with such a swell group of folks. Poke trotted over and lifted a leg on the rear tire of her truck. I cringed.

"Is that your dog?" Lucy's smile was dazzling.

"Yeah. I'm trying to get rid of him."

"He's cute."

"Not when you get to know him. But hey, you want me to handle that auger for you? We could use a few more rods set up." The law allowed six rods per person, but we'd run out of ambition after hand drilling three holes apiece. Updike and I took turns with the power auger and opened a dozen new holes in nothing flat. Lucy walked along behind, scooping slush out of holes and baiting hooks.

"You really enjoy this, huh?" I watched her kneel beside one of the holes, her hand on the line, waiting for a strike. "I mean, Paul said you'd come, but I didn't think you would. It's not like we're overrun with, um, women out here." I looked around. Here and there men swathed in Hollowfill peered sullenly at unmoving rods. "You know, most people would rather be shopping. Not that shopping is all that much fun sometimes, especially if you're broke and you can't buy anything. Especially when it's cold like this. We've got some beer on the sled, though, if you want some. But it's probably frozen."

"That's okay." Suddenly, Lucy's hand shot into the air. She flung her mittens down and yanked her line in, and in moments a perch lay thrashing beside the hole, spanking slush on her parka. The reporter zoomed in for a shot. Over the next two hours, Lucy caught several more, and Updike and I both asked her to land them two or three times while we shot pictures. But it was a slow day, and by noon we had only two dozen fish among the four of us. The reporter packed her gear in the trunk of her car, waved, and drove away. Shortly afterwards, Updike and I decided to leave also.

I asked Lucy if she wanted to have lunch with us. Updike would be happy to foot the bill.

"Oh, no. I think I'll stay out here a little longer. They may start running in an hour or two."

Back at the overlook, I shaded my eyes and scanned the reservoir. Lucy was still out there, a spark of crimson walking from one hole to the next, nudging rod tips with her boot.

"Jesus, she was beautiful," I said.

"I told you she was. Too bad for you she's got a boyfriend."

"Let me know if he dies. And hand me that six-pack. We'll stick them under the heater on the way home."

*   *   *

106

Denver Bryan is a photographer, and that winter his work took him to Canyon Ferry for a session with local ice boaters. He asked me if I wanted to go along. There was a small fleet on the north end of the reservoir, not a great spot for ice fishing, but I decided to throw my buckets and sled in the truck anyway.

I'd seen an occasional boater from the south end of the lake, flying through the squads of fishermen, then tacking upwind, north to where the ice was smoother. I wondered how fast they could go.

When Denver and I pulled in, there were two or three boaters already there, making last-minute adjustments. One man fiddled with a sail and waved.

Denver introduced us. The man was in his sixties and had been an ice boater for decades. He offered me a ride later, when they'd finished with the photo session. I told him I'd love to, that right now I had some fish to catch anyway. I walked a quarter mile out on the ice, bored a half dozen holes—the ice was thinner up here, for some reason—then sat on an overturned bucket to watch the show. Although the wind came in gusts that skittered my tackle across the ice, the day was considerably warmer than the previous outing. Slate clouds scudded overhead.

But the perch weren't biting, although two college kids fifty yards away pulled in trout after trout. Trout aren't nearly as tasty as perch, so I throw mine back, much to the consternation of friends.

More boaters had arrived, and one by one they pushed off, swung downwind, and shot away. I wandered back to watch. Denver was riding with the man I'd met earlier. A few minutes later the two of them coasted to a stop, and Denver hopped off, his eyes wide open behind his glasses. He'd been on an ancient jalopy built of two-by-fours and plywood, with a stout wooden mast and runners of hammered and filed metal fence posts. Hardly a thoroughbred.

"Wait till you try *this*," Denver said.

The squat little boat tugged at its tether, prancing in the hands of its owner. He motioned me over. "You ever done this before?"

"Nope."

"Then just hold on," he said. I climbed in and lay face down beside him, clinging to the front of the platform with both hands. The boat leaped away and instantly raced downwind. I stared at the ice rushing below, twelve inches from the very teeth my parents spent years paying to straighten. Wind bellowed through the sail.

"How fast you think we're going?" My eyes rained tears, and flecks of ice burned my cheeks.

"Probably only thirty," he shouted. The boat swung into the wind.

Only thirty? He was tacking back to shore now, then clicking to a stop. I slid off the platform and wobbled back to my rods. Not a single one had so much as twitched. There I stood, my back to the wind, trying to juxtapose pure, visceral speed with the near cataleptic stasis of standing, forever waiting, over a six-inch hole in the ice. When Denver returned a half hour later, my thoughts poured out: blah blah blah blah ice fishing; blah blah blah blah ice boat; blah blah blah blah goddamn perch. I hadn't caught a thing. Denver tossed me a new jacket and borrowed a trout from the college kids so he could take pictures of me yanking it in and out of the water. Nine months later, I appeared in a full-page spread in a clothing catalogue, for which I received a two hundred dollar gift certificate. I used it to buy a paddling jacket one size too small.

In March, perch move to shore to spawn. At times you might find a school in just two feet of water, and for me, at least, the temptation to lie on the ice and peer at the muck on the bottom is irresistible. But I've yet to see a fish, although I know they can see *me*. Perch are invisible.

Eric Wiltse harbors no such desires, for he is a trout fisherman who, like all trout fishermen on Canyon Ferry Reservoir, rarely catches trout. We had a six-pack of Schmidt beer between us (in the spring the cans feature a leaping musky or bass, making it a favorite of true outdoorsmen), so off we went one fine day with Poke along for the ride. Poke squealed and whined throughout the two-hour drive.

Poke's to be forgiven for his manners, though I've threatened to throttle him more than once. He's a bird dog, and truck rides mean he's going hunting, regardless of how many ice rods are stashed back there with him. Upon our arrival, he shot out of the truck and was halfway across the reservoir before he realized he'd been duped. This would be just another stint of quality time with the boss, something he despises.

But it wasn't a bad day. In the spring, on the few sunny days the wind doesn't blow, the reservoir can be almost pleasant. Wiltse and I stripped to our sweaters and cracked open beers, drained them, and flung the empties on the bank.

Just kidding, you California guys. It appeared we had the

reservoir almost to ourselves, not a good sign. A quarter mile out, one lone ice fisherman poked at a couple of rods, then sat on a bucket shielded by a blue tarp. To the south, two or three fishermen gathered around a pickup, which, unbelievably, someone had driven onto the melting ice.

Several years earlier, I'd driven past a pair of ice fishermen on Ennis Lake, en route to a late March session of fly-fishing on the Madison River. The lake had nearly thawed, and the two of them had walked on spongy ice to the edge of a lead, plunked down stools, and dropped lines through holes drilled twenty yards from open water. Even in Montana, that type of suicidal behavior gets noticed, and I seriously considered calling someone in to tie them up. We went fishing instead, and when we returned they were gone. Drowned? I hope so.

Wiltse and I, having no clue to where there might be fish so late in the year, walked out fifty yards and decided to tough it out right there. We drilled right into the middle of a school.

Here, at last, was something for my bored springer to do. He ran from fish to fish, scooping up each one in his mouth and looking at me. Did I want this one back? Would I mind terribly if he chewed its head off? He quit after awhile and wandered off, in search of anything on the miles of flat ice he could lift his leg on.

Meanwhile, Wiltse and I were having a field day. It was unusual to find a school so soon. Wiltse forgot about trout for the time being and scooted from rod to rod, his fingers on the line, tensed for the strike. Around us lay dozens of perch, most still flopping. Every few seconds one of us would yank a rod high in the air and furiously hand-line in another little fish. It was a fine way to close out the season. Within days the

110

ice would break up, cracking off floes the size of boxcars that would jostle from one side of the reservoir to the other.

By the time the action slowed we'd both had enough. I reeled in lines while Wiltse stowed gear in my sled. When all was in order, he straightened and looked around, then turned toward me. "Where's your dog?" he said.

I squinted across the lake, shielding my eyes from the glare. Poke had disappeared. I cupped my hands around my mouth and yelled. Up the shoreline, perhaps a half mile away, I saw a brown speck pop over a ridge of gravel and gallop my way. "There he is," I said. "He must have been looking for a tree." When he was halfway back, he pivoted toward the center of the reservoir and angled away. He'd spotted the other ice fisherman.

"Poke!"

The man seemed to have disappeared. Poke ran on.

"Poke! No!" I started trotting after him. Poke churned toward the blue tarp. He was less than a hundred yards from it when I saw a head peek out from the side. The man looked at the dog, then at me, with a quizzical expression. Suddenly he sprang from his seat. I saw him reach for a chunk of ice just as Poke skidded to a stop at the farthest of his two rods. The man screamed and threw.

The chunk pinged into the ground between the springer's legs and skipped away. Poke watched it go, dropped his leg, and trotted back to me, happily wagging his tail while the man behind him fumed and held his drenched rod with the tips of his fingers. I waved at him feebly, then walked back to Wiltse, who was grinning. "Season's over," I said.

COUNTRY
MUSIC

This morning I watched a squat, bald man in a navy-blue business suit plunge a pitchfork into a bale of alfalfa. Wedges of hay sloughed off like sections of a croissant, one of which he flipped to a pair of quarter horses. The horses live next door on the Bar Eagle "Ranch," a one-acre spread of fenced dandelions that surround a plywood lean-to and pole corral. As near as I can tell, the horses stay in the corral, period. The man tossed more hay to the horses, then tiptoed through the manure to a waiting van, a soul redeemed from three-martini lunches. Is this a real cowboy? Here under our large sky the suburbs are alive with the sound of George Strait, and sometimes it's hard to tell.

I have learned to enjoy country and western music on its own terms, not mine, because for many, many years all I could get on my truck was an AM country station. Once I also got an oldies station, but the radio went on the fritz and that was that. I felt as though it had willfully undergone a partial laryngectomy, and its treachery stabbed at my heart. My roommate, the first in a succession of surly transients, had a VCR but no stereo, so I was stuck. I had sold my own stereo before I moved up here.

But I've adjusted. Although it's hard to come to terms with the nasal wails of the Porter Wagoner era, I have learned, to my chagrin, that country music is big business these days. This is not news to its artists, most of whom were born in tar-paper shacks in Appalachia, and who nevertheless have parlayed their barefoot days into the big time. Believe it or not, there's rhyme and meter to all this, and it grows on you.

On the other hand, I've always liked Merle Haggard, but

Buck Owens is pushing things. I can't account for this except that Buck Owens was a regular on "Hee Haw," a C&W variety show consummated over the dead bodies of all who stand for sensible and intelligent television programming. When the show finally went off the air the bib overall set must have sighed with relief. With corn prices in the toilet and Nixon in the White House, they'd had enough.

Today, as I shop at Safeway, country muzak wafts between the rows of diet salad dressing and Rice-a-Roni. Later, "Country Countdown" lifts above a fog of nitrous oxide as the dentist hacks at my gums. It seems that to get real country music these days, you have to go to a bar.

Thirty years ago, the club down the road fronted the last whorehouse in the Gallatin Valley. But long before the prefab log homes moved in up the street, the cathouse went out of business, as have so many other American institutions of late. I doubt if the place has changed much since then; above the plank flooring, black-and-white photographs of bronc and bull riders still line the walls, curled and yellow inside their chipped frames. The only color photograph is of bull rider Jim Shoulders and his pet Brahma, Buford T. Lite, autographed by Shoulders himself. Above the pool table in the back, there's a photo of a buffalo dashing off a twenty-foot tower into a pool of water. Why would a buffalo do this? You have to wonder how deep the water is.

The ranchers and their hands are the first to arrive, and from late afternoon on they squat on the stools nearest the door. Like cowboys everywhere, they keep their hats on and their long sleeves buttoned at the cuff. In one corner sits a

116

loner in full regalia—silk scarf, pearl snap shirt, walrus mustache, and full-length canvas slicker. He sips on a Budweiser, frowning beneath a tan Resistol.

Several young women have clustered near the jukebox, chatting among themselves, studiously avoiding looking at the men perched ten feet away. One, a woman in tight red Wranglers and high-heeled boots, has the taut thighs of a figure skater and the face of Emmylou Harris. It's hard not to stare.

I order a beer from the bartender, a woman the size of a dirigible.

"Who's playing tonight?" I ask, nodding toward the musicians on stage.

"Montana Rose."

"Where they from?"

"Don't know."

The Montana Rose Band is definitely country. The bassist has shoulder-length hair and a mustache, and he's flanked by a drummer who has tied his blond hair back in a ponytail. I like ponytails; they're as much the trademark of rednecks as radicals in these modern times, and you can check the roster of the NRA on that one. During moments of rebellion, I've thought of growing one myself. I may still. It's a free country.

I've seen the guitar player before; later I learn that he and the drummer are sitting in with the group for the weekend. The singer is striking—a handsome rather than pretty woman, with high cheekbones and a brief profile. In the orange floodlights she looks part Indian, and may well be of that blood. She likes the song they're about to play, she says; her husband the bass player sang it to her on the night they

117

married. For just a moment the chatter in the bar subsides while the drummer counts the backbeat. Then the bass thumps and music surges through the speakers, and couples edge onto the dance floor. Since that night I've tried to recall that first song. Was it Haggard? McEntire? But I cannot remember anymore than I can forget that woman's voice. How could she have lived to have sung like that?

Within an hour the place is jumping. College students from the university in town have been filtering in for most of the night, and promptly at eleven a squad of businessmen and their wives arrive. The dance floor ripples with the choreographed spinning of couples, the arms of the men pumping to the backbeat. As always, I watch the dancers with a detachment that masks my terror at being asked to dance. But I can dance to rock and roll, I remind myself.

And, in fact, not everyone seems to be enjoying themselves. Some of the men frown with concentration, their dips and spins as preordained as a bad loan. With ranching what it is (and always has been), you'd think they'd find this one little thing to be happy with.

Ah, well. It's easy to coach from the bench. Women flit between jukebox and dance floor, most clinging to broad but short men whose shoulders swell beneath pearl snap shirts. Most are bull riders, limbering up for the rodeo next week. One woman stands with her back to me, tossing back a cascade of platinum hair. As she turns, our eyes meet and she smiles. Then she's off to the dance floor, leaving me straining for another look. Her partner is a good dancer who likes to keep the pace up.

Once upon a time I two-stepped around a barroom floor with a patient gal who didn't mind an occasional pinched toe. As with most of the patient women in my life, I dropped her as though she were rabid. Where is she now? When the music stops the blond drifts to the corner and sits down with the silk-scarfed cowboy I'd seen earlier. Apparently they know each other.

"And now I'd like to do an old Patsy Cline song," the singer says. She smiles at the bass player, taps her foot and eases into "I Fall to Pieces." This cues the less intimate to exit the floor, but a half dozen couples remain, revolving slowly in and out of the glow surrounding the stage. In the corner, the blond rises and extends a hand to the cowboy, and the two of them slide out of the shadows and into the half light.

The blond and I could be happy together. I want to marry a woman like that, a cowgirl with Dura-coat fingernails and flossed teeth. We'd buy a ranch on the West Boulder River. I'd punch cows during the day and two-step on the veranda at night. We'd build a log bunkhouse. We'd raise good bird dogs. We'd be poor but there would always be food on the table, and our children would be secure in our love.

Above the music the singer's voice carries, and one by one the people in the bar pause to listen. The dancers slow and then shuffle in place, and the bartender leans against the counter, her bulldog arms braced against the rail. Heads swivel toward the stage. As the music fades, the woman's voice ascends, singular and fine, and when at last she drops her gaze there is a momentary vacuum as everyone in the room sucks in his breath. Then the walls come apart. "Why, that just gave me goose bumps," the bartender says.

Never could I have danced to *that*.

When the blond walks back to the corner her cowboy follows, and draped down the back of his slicker, like a zipper on the wrong side of his coat, is a braided ponytail. Who would have guessed?

MY TRUCK,
MY DOG,
AND ME

Twenty-five miles east of Manhattan, Montana, lie the Bridger Mountains, which peek through the massive silver poplars shading the trailer court next door. Should take me about forty-five minutes to get to the top of the pass, maybe longer considering the car I'm driving, a 1980 Toyota pickup with 227,000 hard miles on the odometer, one of the few things on the vehicle that still works. The pass is the highest point between my tiny former lineman's shack in Manhattan and my parents' home in southern Iowa.

From up on top it's all downhill and prairie forever. Down through Livingston and across the Yellowstone River where, each winter, the wind flips semitrailers as easily as it tears mittens from the hands of children. From the bridge, I-90 climbs out of the Yellowstone Valley, leveling off between the Crazy and Absaroka mountains, north and south. Then east, across the high plains, where the deer and the antelope play. By Columbus the mountains have disappeared, and it will be the last I see of them for the next ten days. Soon I pass through Laurel and its oil refineries, then sight Shotgun Willies, one of the state's few strip joints and the unofficial beginning of Billings. The interstate meanders northeast, skirting the stinking refineries and welding shops on the south end of town, and then, as if even it too had had enough, takes a hard right into the clean, hot grass of the Crow Indian Reservation. South of Hardin, I keep an eye open for sharptail grouse, which sail back and forth across the interstate. Sharptails are in no danger of extinction, but there aren't as many as there used to be, and it is by these birds that I measure the wild left in the land between the Rockies and the Missouri River. But the sharptails are not moving early this

July morning, because it's too damn hot. Pushing a hundred in Iowa, my mother had quietly said; thank God your father is in an air-conditioned hospital. Still, you'd better come home.

The high plains may be the largest relatively undeveloped region left in the contiguous forty-eight states. Much of this land is every bit as wild as the mountains to the west; one gravel road may be fifty miles from the next, and chill factors in eastern Montana, Wyoming, and North and South Dakota plunge to fifty below every January. Its beauty, and much of it *is* beautiful, is tempered by uncompromising reality: The cold can kill you, and the wind will make you crazy. A few years ago, a former roommate of mine walked away from a head-on collision near Mosby, Montana, and vanished in the sagebrush. She's been sighted since at truck stops across the top of the country, a wisp of strawberry-blond hair in a dark booth, a fugitive from her own sanity.

My travels through this land, traced on a map, would look like the doodlings of a kid with a crayon in his paw: circle upon circle upon circle. One loop, heavily indented, would swing due south through John Gierach's creaking bungalow in northern Colorado, and another would angle southeast toward Dave Reed's little farmhouse in the wooded hills of northwestern Missouri. On this trip, I looped through Sundance, Wyoming, where I stopped long enough to water Rabbit, my English setter puppy who was making the trip with me, and spent ten minutes trying to call another old roommate, whom the operator had never heard of. So I filled up my coffee cup and hit the road again. I was hoping to make Mitchell, South Dakota, by dark.

124

Sundance is on the edge of the Black Hills, a series of rolls larger than normal in country that is more rolling than flat. Anywhere east of the Missouri they'd be considered mountains, but not here, with the Rockies a day's drive to the west. From Montana to Omaha the land heaves, rolls, and finally flattens, like the graph on a heart monitor signing off. With typical government penchant for the bland, however, most of the highways that traverse this region stick to the flats, which certain rural folks have gone to extremes to deny: Outside of New Salem, North Dakota, just south of the interstate, is a fiberglass Holstein three stories tall, a stirring monument to ennui. It works, though. You can't ignore the thing.

I stayed on I-90 through Wall, South Dakota, stopping for gas in the Dino station outside of town, where an ancient codger in tan coveralls peered at me through a filthy plate-glass window. He rose creaking from his chair when I walked inside to pay. "Hot, ain't it?" he said.

I nodded. A furnace-like blast of wind buffeted the structure, slamming the door shut.

"Goddamn thing," he said. "Supposed to hit a hundred to-day."

"I believe it. Say, what's this Wall Drug stuff I keep reading about? The billboards? Is that here somewhere?"

"It's here. You just keep on going the way you come and turn left up there at the grocery store. You'll run right into it."

The cash register clanged open and he scooped out my change.

In fact, the place was impossible to miss. People streamed down wooden sidewalks, or clustered around shop windows.

Children screamed. I veered off on a side road and parked beneath a cottonwood that afforded shade for the dog, then set off on foot toward the center of town. Wall Drug, I found, was like a half dozen other Western-theme tourist traps I'd visited: cute and overly rustic. I poked around a mall for fifteen minutes, then turned for the door. Almost out, I stepped into a narrow hallway that branched away, unnoticed, from the throngs of tourists. The walls of the hallway were papered with snapshots. There was the founder of Wall Drug, his sons, grandchildren, and friends. And over there, a strikingly handsome soldier in a World War II army uniform. Entire families smiling into the lens. A senator. Movie stars. Men posing with mule deer and antelope; boys with their .22s. Three generations of men and women from black and white to color. As always, I was drawn in, lost in the scalloped-edged black and whites. Who were these people? Were they still alive? Were they happy?

As I gazed at a group of dark-haired kids, I recalled a similar photo, a snapshot printed on the same Kodak Velox paper, a picture my mother had taken of me as a child. In it I'm smiling proudly at the camera, dressed head to toe in a tiny khaki army uniform, a toy rifle at parade rest. A helmet hides my red hair. Behind me, slightly out of focus, is the tractor tire that served as my sandbox. This must have been '60, maybe '61. Sometime around then—I would have been five or six—my father brought me a box turtle he'd caught in the sandhills of Nebraska. We put the turtle in the sandbox, where it survived for the two or three days it took our German shepherd to find it. I seem to remember burying the

126

turtle under the weeping willow in the backyard, but maybe dad just threw it away.

Just at dark, I crossed the Missouri River impoundment, Lake Francis Case, near Chamberlain, and chugged up the bluffs overlooking the lake on the east side. I pulled into a rest stop and killed the engine. Beside me, Rabbit yawned and sat up, staring idly out the windshield. The reservoir stretched north and south as far as I could see, lights blinking softly from the water. I'd nearly forgotten it was the Fourth of July, and dozens of boats had anchored around the bridge to watch the fireworks display. Other cars were parked in the rest stop, watching the show. I stepped outside, stretched, and was besieged by mosquitoes. In the rest room I scrubbed the grime and insects from my face, then dashed back to the car, praying the bugs wouldn't follow me for the hour it would take to get to Mitchell. They didn't.

Mitchell is home to the Corn Palace, which, like North Dakota's leviathan Holstein, was probably conceived in a fit of economic desperation. Most travelers, like me, would not detour cross country to gaze upon an auditorium laminated with several million kernels of corn, but the place no doubt sucks in a few. In any event, it was closed when I got there, so I pulled into a restaurant halfway through town, and after watering the dog again, stepped inside.

After I'd ordered, a smiling young woman brought me dinner: a leathery wafer of chicken-fried steak, flung on my plate like a dare. I choked it down, paid my bill, and left, looking for a place to spend the night.

When sleeping in pickups, avoiding cops—and a two A.M.

127

suggestion to rent a motel room or leave town—is a matter of finding someplace they either don't look or don't care about. Eventually, I discovered a vacant lot behind a racetrack, and after letting Rabbit romp around a few minutes, rolled out my sleeping bag. By force of habit, I searched for the North Star, which my father, once an Air Force navigator, had shown me as a boy. There it was, twinkling to beat the band, the Little Dipper slowly twirling round. I fell asleep to the whine of traffic on the interstate.

July fifth dawned blistering hot, and I awoke sweating in my bag, the upper half unzipped and flung from my chest. After filling the tank at a station on the edge of town, I swung back into traffic on I-90. The rolls and buttes of the prairie had disappeared late the previous afternoon, and from here on in was farmland, some of the most fertile in the world. In Sioux Falls, South Dakota, I turned straight south on I-29, heading toward Sioux City, Iowa, and the wooded bluffs bordering the Missouri River.

Southeast of Sioux City, the interstate eased away from the Missouri and into miles of rustling corn, then gradually swung back south again, as if drawn to the river. Near Onawa, it skirted the Loess Hills, an ancient, sedimentary deposit of windblown silt, then passed through a half dozen one-horse towns before connecting with I-80 north of Council Bluffs. I was five miles south of Onawa, making time, when the Toyota's water pump blew.

I've never suffered mechanical breakdowns lightly, and now my pulse went through the roof. Three hours from home! I stormed around the ticking vehicle, slamming my fist again and again into the hood. When I finally calmed enough to think, I stowed everything I could in the cab, clipped the puppy to a leash, and sat on the tailgate, hitching a ride. It was hellishly hot. Rabbit sprawled behind my legs, panting, seeking what little shade I provided. I pulled my cowboy hat over my eyes and stuck out my thumb, hailing passing cars with curses. A half hour later, hot, miserable, and utterly discouraged, I heard a voice from behind me.

A man waved from a pickup on the frontage road paralleling the highway. I trotted down the borrow pit to the barbed wire fence that separated us.

"You need some help?" he said.

"Do I ever! Let me lock the car!" I tied Rabbit's leash to the fence, loped back to the truck, and returned a moment later. My rescuer was in his sixties, trim for a man his age. He lifted a tackle box off the floorboard and stowed it between us. Behind the seat were several strung spinning rods. "My name's Jim Joines," he said.

I took his hand. "Dave Carty. Something's wrong with my truck, I'm not sure what. The fan is wobbling all over the place, and it makes noise when I drive."

"Sounds like the water pump."

"Is that serious?" I sagged into the seat, the dog between my legs. The air-conditioning in the cab was heaven; it was hard to believe I'd driven this far without it.

"Depends. I'll tell you what. I know a guy down at the Texaco that'll fix you right up. He does all my work for me, and he's fair. He can probably come out here and tow you in, but if not, I can do it with the truck."

"Jesus, I'd appreciate that. I'm supposed to be home right now—my parents live south of Des Moines—but then this. I'll

129

be happy to pay for the gas you use, whatever. I really didn't know what I was going to do out there."

He shrugged. "Don't worry about it," he said.

Joines was right; my water pump had gone out, and the station didn't have a replacement. But the Toyota dealership in Sioux City did, and he volunteered to drive me there. It was a forty-minute trip, so we talked.

After a career in the Navy, Joines had settled in Iowa, building himself a home from the ground up. I told him I was doing the same in Montana, one stick at a time. "You have any help at all?" he asked.

There'd been some, I told him; one friend had stuck it out through the foundation and most of the walls. But now that the project was into its second year, help was getting hard to find. My friends had lives and projects of their own.

"Hell," Jim said, "my own family got fed up. It's pretty hard not to, once they figure out how much work it's going to take." He chuckled. "Took me three years. But I finally got it done. I think everybody should build a house at least once. That's it over there, behind those trees." He pointed west, toward the Missouri. "I planted all of those ten years ago. Never could figure out why people would live someplace without trees."

"You got that right," I said. I'd already planted nearly 250 trees on the two acres I owned.

Near Sioux City, the interstate skirted the bank of the river. Joines had fished all of it. Catfish, he said, were the best goddamn eating fish anywhere.

"In fact," he told me, "I sort of invented this rig." He fished through his tackle box and pulled out a simple hook and wire

130

arrangement, steering with his elbows while he demonstrated how it worked. Rabbit watched from the floorboards. "I wanted to put it into production or something, but I haven't got around to that yet. Mostly I fish and canoe. It's real nice, out there on the river."

A few years earlier, Joines had been told by his doctors he was going to die. "I was ready to go," he said. "I figured that was it. They said I had cancer, that there wasn't much they could do. I wasn't real happy about it, but you finally accept it after awhile. How old did you say your dad was?"

"He turned sixty-six last week."

"Well, he's a little older than me, but not by much. So anyway, turns out they were wrong. I wasn't going to die after all. Bad diagnosis." Joines hit the blinker and swung onto a ramp that entered Sioux City. "But it makes you appreciate things, believe me."

By early that afternoon, Joines had not only taken me to Sioux City, but back to Onawa again, towing my truck in en route.

The mechanic at the station had the old pump out and the new one in in no time, and I was ready for the road by two. I copied Joines's address onto a scrap of paper, thanked him for the dozenth time, and drove out of the dank garage into the still searing heat.

The remainder of the trip took a little over the three hours I'd estimated. I arrived to an empty house, but there was a spare key in the garage, as my mother had told me there would be. The phone was ringing as I unlocked the door. When I picked up the receiver I heard my youngest sister

131

Patty's frantic voice. Had I seen mom? Was she on her way to the hospital? Evidently, my mother had told her to meet her there as soon as she could, then left herself. But mom had disappeared.

I placed the phone back on the hook and collapsed into a chair at the kitchen table, staring out the sliding glass door at the heat waves dancing across the patio. Within minutes the phone rang again. It was Patty. Mom was at the hospital, with her. Dad was dead. Worn out from a year of constant pain, his wasted heart and kidneys shot, he'd simply given up.

For the remainder of the week I couldn't keep Rabbit in the house. She'd charge across the room, knocking over my mother's antiques, cringing when touched. I finally had to chain her in the front yard, where she cried until I drove to Dave Reed's farmhouse in Missouri the following week. She didn't settle down completely until we left, cutting back on I-80 across utterly flat Nebraska, skirting the south edge of the sandhills and then north, bound for the prairie.

ROAD
WARRIOR

With all the broken, endless miles of public land in Montana, I can no more hunt out my back door than I can swim to the moon. There are not, for instance, Hungarian partridge and pheasants living under my porch. Nice thought, though.

The best bird hunting in the state—the locations of which have already been sprayed, ad infinitum, across the pages of the hook and bullet journals—is a good three hours north of my humble little squatter's shack in Manhattan, where I live in violation of city ordinances with one bird dog over the two-dog limit. A day's drive will put you in even better country up toward North Dakota, or thoroughly lost somewhere around Fort Peck Reservoir in the northeast corner of the state. Every now and then, someone will head out toward Fort Peck and disappear, never to be seen again. A few days later his car will turn up, its doors open and creaking in the wind, a note pinned to the dash with a straightened paper clip. Or maybe not. I wonder about these things.

But that's not going to happen to *me*. I know my way around. Furthermore, I've learned to cope with the endless hours spent behind the wheel of my 1980 Toyota pickup with 200,000-plus big ones on the odometer, the scud missile of Japanese trucks. There's a kennel in the back for the dogs, and the camper shell has windows that won't shut, so the dogs can poke their noses out and freeze to death in the winter, which they seem to enjoy. My Toyota isn't going to run forever, but for the time being, it's giving it the old college try.

*   *   *

135

A couple seasons ago, James Goosen, a newspaper man newly arrived in Billings, gave me a call. Goosen had been told to contact me by a mutual friend in Colorado. With the season nearly over, he was hoping to catch up on his bird hunting, and was I interested in heading out for a day? I was, and we made a date to meet at my place the following weekend. He arrived on a Friday evening, and that night we sat up until late drinking wine and discussing options. The option we eventually decided upon was to stop drinking wine before we fell over, and the next day head north to a ranch I'd lined up, three hours away.

At four thirty the following morning we staggered around my house gathering gear and duffelbags, still hurting from the two bottles of wine we'd drunk. Our ever-helpful dogs slapped happy tongues across our faces whenever we sagged against the sofa to rest, and then, when we arose, ran shrieking to the front door. This was hard to take so early on the day of our big adventure, but we eventually got all three animals—James's ailing Lab and my Brittany and springer—into the back of the Toyota and pointed it east toward Livingston for the first leg of our trip.

Just up the road, traffic slowed to a crawl and then stopped altogether as road crews removed rocks from the interstate, whether from a slide or construction we never learned. This did nothing to improve our mood, and James groaned. I spun the dial on the radio, and finally tuned in an AM gospel hour, the only entertainment I could find. The preacher ranted while we fumed, but the jam didn't break for another half hour, well after the sun had come up. Moved, we bowed our heads in prayer:

O Lord, let there be scads of Hungarian
partridge in thy wheat fields, and let our
dogs' points be true. Forsake not those in
thy Toyotas, and visit not upon us your
wealthy evangelists of the radio, who
taketh their congregations to the cleaners
and payeth not their taxes, amen.

Just outside of Harlowton, the truck started missing. I pulled onto the shoulder, popped the hood, and fiddled with the spark plug wires. "Fiddled" is an exact description, since I did nothing but wiggle the wires and shove the spark plug sockets farther onto the heads of the plugs. This is a routine I have developed all by my unmechanical self, since the car invariably won't act up when I take it to a mechanic, and since I don't have the slightest idea of what else to do. In fact, I'm a helpless spastic with engines of any sort. But when I fired up the Toyota it ran just fine, as I suspected it would for about the next twenty minutes, or until the sun rose high enough to dry out the humid air. We reached the small ranch we planned to hunt around ten, nearly five hours after we had left, two hours longer than planned. And there, a place that over the years had provided one superb hunt after another, we put up just one covey of Huns, and I killed two of the three birds we took on two consecutive rises. This was not to be James's day, and nearly every bird we saw that morning rose directly in front of me. So at noon it was back into the truck and east down the highway, over the iron trestle spanning the shallow Judith River, and up the incline on the other side, swerving around the potholes. Before we retired the season, there was another spot I knew about just up the road. Fourth gear and forty-five minutes and we'd be there.

137

*   *   *

Prior to my annual trip to Iowa last year, I bought a tape deck, my first ever. I never made it to Iowa, and the truth is that I've made it only twice in the last five years, which probably stretches the definition of the word "annual," but there you are. That was just as well, because the tape deck never made it through the installation into the dash, dying on the operating table, so to speak. I took it back to K mart and got another one. A week later I drove north to Spokane to pick up two setter puppies, one for me, one for a friend.

I'd just sunk $150 into miscellaneous repairs, including a tune-up, and the truck purred. I could hardly believe I could drive for two days—seven hours each way—with no major mechanical troubles. Coming home, I passed through Coeur d'Alene, Idaho, then Smelterville (bar none, the West's ugliest town), and shortly afterwards precipitous Wallace. It was in Wallace that Hollywood filmed *Heaven's Gate*, the colossal Western that cost umpteen millions to make and that promptly bombed prior to release. Today, Wallace has a new interstate snaking through town, soaring above the houses below on concrete pylons thirty feet high. But Wallace still *looks* like a Western lumber town, a great place to film a movie, a place a friend of mine who grew up there described as having one whorehouse for every two bars.

In Kellogg, Idaho, I stopped in a music store to buy my first tape ever for my first-ever tape deck: "Lyle Lovett and his Large Band." The tape cost eleven dollars, which I thought a bit pricey. But Lyle does a great rendition of "Stand by Your Man," and there is much to recommend country music in a Toyota pickup, where no more than one of your friends

138

at a time has to listen to it. Also, I like to sing along when no one else can hear me, and C&W lyrics are easy to fake if you forget the words. Try this for sparkle:

> My mama was a truck drivin' man,
> She done the best for us she can,
> But the day she married that perfessor,
> I done found out mama was a cross
>   dresser.
>
> (Chorus)
>
> Whoa! Them cheatin' women'll get you
>   down,
> And I'm so lonesome, I could drown.

I've written even better ones than that, but not right off the top of my head. Anyway, you'd be surprised how good it sounds three or four hours into a road trip at the end of a long day, the dogs sacked out in the back, a bag of potato chips half gone on the front seat. Turn up the volume, open the windows, and let 'er rip.

After years of checking off equipment against a list, it finally dawned on me that it would be easier to store it all in a duffel bag and keep it with my shotgun, vest, and water bottle, ready for a quick foray into the hinterlands. The plan has worked wonderfully, and has mostly eliminated forgotten items (I'm the only person I know who regularly forgets the list of things I wrote down to remind me of things not to forget). The new and improved list is shorter and much easier to remember, a refrain I mumble to myself that sounds almost like a chant: gunsvestwaterduffeldogs. I still forget money on occasion, especially when I have friends along, which, heh, heh, forces them to pay for gas. But seriously, they enjoy hunting with a famous writer.

On the last day of the season, I usually head off by myself, up toward the head of the Shields Valley, a scant hour's drive away. Last year, however, I was invited to hunt in central Montana with Bill Garges, a hospital appliance rep from Missoula. Into the back of the truck went the gunsvestwaterduffeldogs, and into the front of the truck went I. Once over Bozeman Pass, the local stations faded and I tuned in to the C&W station in Livingston, the town just over the hill.

East of the pass, on the long, downhill run to the Yellowstone River, the wind howls day and night and abandoned windmills, erected prior to the Reagan administration's ban on sensible energy use, topple over on an irregular basis. This is fine country, and the draws and hilly wheat fields on either side of the interstate have always looked birdy to me. In fact, there probably are a few sharptail grouse scattered about, but there have never been many this high up and this far west, which is why I am, once again, in my truck heading elsewhere.

There was no traffic jam this time around, so I shot down the interstate to Big Timber, then up 191 toward Eddie's Corner. For December, it was mild, almost balmy. In less than two weeks, the temperature would plummet to thirty below, then hover well below zero for another two weeks. But at that moment it was hard to imagine better weather for the dogs—highs in the forties, some damp to the ground, perfect scenting conditions for my little Brittany, Fancy, whom I'd

140

brought up front with me. Fancy is a C&W fan herself, so I slid Lyle into the tape deck.

Central Montana is not for everyone. Wheat fields run to the horizon, the only visual relief the shimmering, purple incline of the Little Belts to the west. The town of Judith Gap, which sits squarely in the center of central Montana, is hammered by winds that roll off the slopes of the Little Belts, bellow across miles of uninterrupted wheat stubble, and slam up against the handful of frame homes in town. Not everyone who lives there will put up with that indefinitely, and some leave for bigger towns, which is almost any town anywhere else in the country. But a sense of place runs deep in rural folk, and a few, after having left for years or decades to earn more money elsewhere, return and live out their lives in the place they were born.

When we shot through Judith Gap a warm sun glowed evening red. I stopped the truck, stepped out, and looked around. For once, there was no wind. For some inexplicable reason, I love this country, and there was much out here I had yet to see. But exploration would have to wait; Bill and his two Brittanies were expecting me for dinner.

Back in the truck, I ran the needle up to sixty and rolled down the window, then cranked up the volume on the tape deck. When Lyle segued into "Stand by Your Man," I jumped in on the chorus. I can sing with the best of them sometimes, I really believe I can. God, it was glorious. And just an hour more to go.

WALKING
THE DOG

Manhattan, Montana, is an itsy-bitsy place, just eleven hundred people last count. I can easily walk from one end to the other, which is precisely what I do Monday through Friday mornings, shortly after arising from bed. I walk because I can no longer run, having some time ago left the ligaments of my favorite knee in the trash can under an operating table. For that misfortune I blame ten years as a fairly good skier with a great skier's lunatic insistence that my bindings not release.

In any event, once the dogs are out of the house and safe in their kennel, I'm motivated. I head south first, coaxing cold muscles into an easy rhythm, hitting my stride as I round the first corner two blocks away. Then it's straight east to Taylor Park, with its log gazebo and softball diamonds. North and then west to the city maintenance buildings, where I keep an eye open for Stuart, the city handyman whose two boxers once threatened to chew off my ankles. The pair ride side by side in his truck, sizing up pedestrians as though they were buckets of fried chicken.

Most of the time I make it over the railroad tracks ahead of the train, which rumbles through around eight o'clock. If not, I'll rock from one leg to the other, staring at the wheels of the boxcars as the ground trembles under my feet, wondering for the thousandth time what it would be like to hop a freight just for the hell of it.

Immediately beyond the tracks lies old Manhattan, or at least that section of town visible in a 1921 photo on display in the bank. These homes, like nearly every other home in town, are immaculate, with the neatly painted siding and manicured yards characteristic of the other Dutch farming communities in the area: Churchill to the south, and tiny Amsterdam to the southwest.

On the north side of town, bordering old Manhattan, are newer homes. One is owned by Marian, formerly one of the valley's more eligible gals, recently removed from the social milieu by a new husband. At thirty-nine, Marian still looks drop-dead gorgeous in the checkered shorts she wears to present trophies at the Hub of the Valley stock-car track. She tells me she's seen me walking from across the way, and asked once why I didn't wave. I didn't wave, I told her, because from across the way, all I could see was the blue reflection of sky on her picture window. But every few days I glance over there, and if the reflection slides or shimmies a bit, I'll raise my hand, feeling like an idiot for waving at a house.

Once past Marian's I hit the old oil road to Belgrade, one of two highways used by locals before the interstate went in. Then, two hundred yards farther, I take a right on Yadon Road, which runs straight north past the grade school to the Gallatin River. Without fail, I'll be passed by a black flatbed bearing a grim man wearing a white Stetson, his yellow Labrador retriever sitting beside him. Neither smiles or waves, notable hereabouts only because almost everyone else does. At the silver poplar tree a quarter mile beyond the grade school, I'll spin on my heel and head back home, past the grade school, high school, and Albertson's Automotive; past the bearded giant of a man smiling under a bowler, clutching a coffee cup in one huge mitt and the tiny hand of his little girl in the other; past the post office and grain elevators; past the Oasis Restaurant and Bar; past Paul, my next-door neighbor

146

who walks to the post office every morning; and finally into the yard of my own little rented shack, my heart rate right up there at 150 beats per minute, almost as good as it used to be when I could run, I keep telling myself.

I've always enjoyed walking, a fondness I share with others of the literati, whose names I can't remember right this moment. Aside from walking as exercise, I walk as recreation, until recently accompanied by one of my three dogs: Fancy, my Brittany; Rabbit, my English setter; and Poke, a.k.a. Shut Up Poke, my crazed springer spaniel.

Rabbit is the newest, just a year old as I write this. This summer she was a tiny little thing, romping around my heels as we walked the gravel streets through town, while Fancy and Poke mournfully watched us disappear from their kennel. But one at a time is all I can handle. Poke and Fancy invariably rocket out of the kennel straight for the highway. To date, Shut Up Poke has been bumped twice and Fancy has had close calls. So far, though, the puppy is staying close at hand, casting out for robins and meadowlarks, then quickly scampering back to my side.

One of my favorite walks is along the Gallatin River, a five-minute drive from home. This is one of the few places I can take all three dogs, letting them crash through the woods while I explore beaver ponds and river channels. Thanks to team sports as a youngster, I have to install a brace on my right ankle, which otherwise will collapse with no warning, sending me sprawling. Still, it's worth the slight discomfort to be out there with the kids. Rabbit, who was learning to swim last summer, would wade out into water up to her chest, then paddle wide-eyed back to shore, and Poke would crouch on

147

the bank, catapulting into the river after the rocks I skipped off the surface. Fancy usually vanished in the willows, perfectly happy hunting on her own.

I bought a pair of rubber boots for walking in wet bottomlands, shin-high outfits some farmers use for irrigating. The boot on my right foot has stretched enough to allow the brace to slide in, and they're fairly comfortable for an hour's walk, provided I don't stay out much longer than that. I usually don't, since within an hour the dogs are covered with burrs. Last spring, one of the wettest since I moved here, the Gallatin roared out of its banks, flooding several hundred yards of willows along both sides. That was just fine with my unsinkable springer, who swam from log jam to tree stump, collecting burrs on his ears as he went.

This Thanksgiving, I visited my mother in Iowa, and thanks to her cooking, I ballooned to 185, ten pounds over my customary weight. I hadn't walked in the week I'd been there, even though Rabbit and Fancy, whom I'd brought with me, were beside themselves with boredom. I'd be visiting an old friend in Missouri in a few days, though, and I hoped to spend time running both of them in the wooded hills surrounding his farm. Poke, who had long ago shown himself unfit for travel by howling for days on end and defecating in unfamiliar kitchens, had been left, despondent, in a kennel in Montana. I almost gave him a call to cheer him up: "I'm having fun, wish you were here," that sort of thing. Is it so strange to want to call your dog?

As it turned out, I ran Fancy and Rabbit for a day and a half in six inches of new, wet snow, which gave them and me more exercise than we had bargained for. They were utterly pooped, and the next day slept the entire twelve hours it took to drive from Missouri to Colorado to visit friends. Unknown to me, while I was in Colorado, Shut Up Poke had taken it on the lam after chewing his way through the chain-link run of his kennel. He made it as far as the first highway, where he was killed by a car. I learned of his death from the distraught owners of the kennel, one hour after my arrival home. I sprinkled his ashes in the snow around my home, wishing I'd called after all.

One of the problems with walking dogs is that dogs don't want to *walk* anywhere. Instead, they run, full tilt, to wherever it is they're going, then run full tilt back to you again, out and back, until they collapse from exhaustion. This endearing trait is common to nearly all dogs, with the exception of Labrador retrievers, which are designed to weigh three hundred pounds. So you see, God has a purpose for all creatures, great and small.

Still, social walks require more restraint than I can now manage with Fancy and Rabbit, now that the latter has grown up. Consequently, I take walks by myself—in town, mostly, on summer evenings, when it's always cool enough for a light jacket, even during July and August. Night walks are rambles, with no destination in mind, a hands-in-the-pockets meander under the elms and green ash trees of Manhattan. Like a thief, I stick to the alleys, which are lined with gardens and open garages, giving me a peek at private lives. I've been caught staring over fences more than once, always an embarrassment. How do I explain I was only looking?

In September, Manhattan is abuzz, as blond Dutchmen

drive truck after sagging truck of seed potatoes through town. I've been told Manhattan is the seed potato capital of the world, and I believe it. But beef is also a going concern. A couple of years ago, the beef industry people filmed a commercial in town, shot partially at the Oasis Restaurant. I may be the only person in the country who hasn't seen it, since I refuse to buy a television set. But for those of you who may have seen it, I live just three blocks west, in the little brown shack the locals call the dollhouse.

Late last October, my morning walks were sorely tested. The Siberian Express arrived a month early, and temperatures plunged to twenty below. Even for those of us used to the cold and snow of the high plains, this was a bit much. The Taylor Park road was snowed in, so I stuck to the main streets in town, walking in the ruts left by passing cars, puffing along wreathed in a cloud of my own breath. By the time I crossed the railroad tracks my thighs had gone numb. Afterwards, they stung for an hour.

The dollhouse, which wasn't insulated at all until ten years ago, and then only marginally, gets cranky in cold weather. Even with the electric baseboards turned as high as I dare, drafts keep the place chilly. The moment the temperature drops below zero, the supply line to the toilet freezes, which is what the bucket next to the tub is for: filled with tap water and poured into the toilet bowl, the toilet reluctantly flushes.

When the inevitable thaw finally arrived, melting snow on the roads formed a murky glaze, making it impossible to walk for any distance at all. I was forced to quit my morning walks until the roads cleared a few days later. Happily, November became progressively warmer right through the Bozeman Christmas stroll, a first.

On December fifth each year, Bozeman hosts an open house throughout the downtown business district. All the shops are open and we, the strolling citizens of the Gallatin Valley, are welcome to tour each in turn. Volunteers in pickups cordon off Main Street, watching hay wagons carting screaming children. High school boys sneak beers in darkened alleys. But those of us in our thirties, male and single, have another reason for making the stroll year after year. It is legend among us that on this night only, every attractive woman in town will appear, parade herself from one end of Main to the other, and vanish from the face of the earth until the next stroll, a long and difficult twelve months later.

This year I made the loop with Chuck Rasmussen and his two boys. Fifteen years ago, Chuck was a ski jumper for Montana State, and then, by turns, married, a professional musician, divorced, and now a full-time father. Women love this tall, slightly balding guy, and I was hoping that whatever it is he has would ooze out of his size-twelve Reeboks and rub off on me.

Chuck's kids—Eric, eight, and Chris, five—are a lot like my dogs—friendly, curious, and cute. Together, the two boys seem to run in three directions at once, so we had our hands full. Chuck bought us cookies from a stand, which slowed them some; but by the time we paused to buy Polish sausages, the boys had darted into the crowd. Chuck looked at me, then toward the opposite side of the street. When he turned to-

151

ward me again they had reappeared at his side, quivering with energy. "Where did you two go?" he asked.

"I don't know! I don't know!" they squeaked. And then they were off again.

While working for a grocery store two years ago, Chuck slipped on a patch of mud and injured his back. He remembers that instant like some veterans remember combat, with crystal clarity: his legs flipping out from under him, he clawing at the air in an attempt to break his fall, and the sickening whomp! as shoulders met concrete. The injury put him out of work, possibly forever. Yet he's remarkably positive about it all, and dotes on his sons. But one hour of easy walking up and down Main Street took its toll, and Chuck informed me, smiling, that he had pain shooting from his hips to his knees. It was time to go. We angled out of the crowd and down a side street toward his car.

"Well Chuck," I said, "another Christmas." Behind us, the tinsel bells swinging above Main sparkled red and gold.

I had bills to pay that month, so for the next week I parked in front of my computer, churning out magazine articles. One evening, halfway through a story, I heard carolers from down the street. As they approached, their voices ascended, wavered, then meshed in imperfect harmony. Fancy and Rabbit bolted up from the floor, staring at the front door. Then Fancy barked in a quavering falsetto, her imitation of Shut Up Poke's hoarse rumble, bless his brave heart. I hit the switch on the computer and watched the monitor go blank, then slid out of my chair and walked to the window.

152

TREES

Long before I'd laid out the foundation for my new home, landscaping was a priority. I wanted trees—hundreds of them if possible—a tall order on the two and a quarter acres of anemic soil I purchased three years ago. My contribution to the ubanization of America was to buy land in a subdivision that had once been a farm. Wheat gave way to olive-green transformers, bare dirt, and red flags when the place was sold to a developer. Eventually mountain brome returned, a durable native grass that grew to my chest last summer, a waving, deceptively thick carpet of green that belied the essential infertility of the soil below it. Or what there was of soil: Eight inches under the baked surface of my lot lay pure river rock, the ancient alluvial deposit of the East Gallatin River. Kevin the well driller, who bored sixty-two feet through what would one day be my front yard, punched through fist-sized rocks every inch of the way. There was simply no end to the stuff.

But there is balance, if not justice, in nature, and the parched soil of my subdivision lay over a veritable lake of sweet groundwater. Kevin hit a gusher: My well had a nearly continuous flow of thirty gallons per minute, enough water to flood my lot even in the heat of August, when the only things still moving are clouds of bulletproof grasshoppers. So don't think it didn't occur to me.

A few days later I put up a power pole, had the driller run a line to the submersible pump, and dove headfirst into the tree business.

Trees are hardly a hobby for an impatient man. Even the "weed" trees—cottonwoods, willows, poplars, dogwoods, and other water lovers, which rocket skyward in comparison to, say, oaks and hickories—grow at best two or three feet a year. Here in God's own subdivision, you can realistically cut that growth rate in half, according to my friend Mary Hansen, who's been fighting Montana's abbreviated growing season for years. Mary delights in puncturing the fiction printed in nursery catalogues. Once, after outlining to her how I'd planted dozens of Scotch pines and cottonwoods, had dug the holes just so, and, per instructions, had flooded the tiny trees before and after transplanting, she'd paused, held a half-empty bourbon glass to the light, and announced they'd all be dead in five years. She was wrong; most of them didn't make it past the first winter.

Nonetheless, I devised a ten-year plan. In one decade I wanted shade, which meant trees I planted as twelve-inch saplings would have ten years to creep a foot or so above my six-foot frame. A reasonable expectation, I thought.

More than shade, however, I wanted privacy. My lot is on the east side of the subdivision, with houses to the north, west, and south. A wooded windbreak bordering three sides of my property would block the view of the other homes in the area and, with an open twenty-acre pasture directly to the east and the looming Bridger Mountains beyond, give my small lot far more visual seclusion than I had paid for.

So the weed trees got the nod for their hardiness, quick growth, and fall color. On the north and west borders of my property I planted a row of Scotch pines, which would provide a screen after the leaves on the deciduous trees had fallen. To the west, inside the pines, I planted two rows of golden willows. Willows are weeds in the truest sense of the word. I'd planned to buy several dozen saplings from my local nurseryman, but he'd tossed me his pruning shears and told me to take cuttings, as many as I wanted. The foot-long twigs would grow once shoved in the ground and watered, he told me. And he was right. That first spring, nearly every cutting sprouted buds, and several sent up shoots six or eight inches long.

I planted two rows of cottonless cottonwoods on the north side of the house, in parallel rows inside the pines. I've always loved cottonwoods, with their furrowed, ancient bark and vibrant autumn foliage of translucent yellow. These too I obtained as cuttings, spending two hours shoving three dozen into the rocky earth.

I also planted two decorative groves in the front yard, mostly aspens, a grove on either side of the well. Although they weren't available that spring, I eventually planned to line the driveway with Rocky Mountain junipers, a wiry little conifer, though slow growing. Between the aspens and future junipers went a row of Russian olives, an equally tough import, which, as an added plus, produce hard brown berries that attract songbirds.

Trees are cheap when you buy rootstock saplings less than a foot in height. I had a few dollars remaining after my major purchases, and splurged on Nanking cherry bushes at a buck apiece. An even half dozen went on the north side of the lot, beside three Russian olives I'd planted at the end of a row of cottonwood cuttings. A final Nanking cherry went into the front yard, just beyond the aspens. I had nowhere else to put it.

By now, I'd planted close to two hundred trees, and there was no way I could water them all by hand. Fortunately, I discovered a cheap, flexible drip irrigation tubing called

T-tape, which came highly recommended by my nurseryman. At six cents a foot, I could buy miles of the stuff, about what I needed. The T-tape wouldn't last forever, I was told; what does? But it would last the four or five years it would take to get the trees established, and by then I might be able to do without supplementary irrigation at all. This was an optimistic prediction, I learned, but at the time it sounded good to me, and I bought fifteen hundred feet of it, including fittings. It took nearly an hour for water to completely fill the lines, but fill they eventually did, allowing one precious drop at a time to percolate through the soil at twelve-inch intervals.

Shortly after the trees were planted I hired out the excavation of my crawl space to a backhoe operator who moonlighted as a drummer in a rock band. A month or two after the excavation I had a foundation and subfloor down, and as soon as the excavator backfilled the foundation, I made plans for a yard.

Although the Rocky Mountain States perennially limp from one drought to the next, Kentucky bluegrass is still the universal choice for lawns, despite the prodigious amount of water it requires. Like a spoiled blond, a bluegrass lawn shows its brown, shallow soul when the money runs out, money across the West roughly equivalent to water. I wanted a lawn that would thrive, or at least get by, with a minimum of fuss. Buffalo grass, a resilient, native prairie grass, qualified, but its bunch-grass growth pattern was unattractive in a formal lawn. The already established mountain brome was also a consideration. One of the neighbors had mowed his to an acceptable height, then watered it until it filled in. But although the brome had thickened, it still didn't look like a lawn; it looked like an acre of mountain brome with a haircut. No lawn at all—the natural look—was also appealing but ultimately impractical, for I needed at least some protection from grass fires.

I finally settled on tall fescue, sold locally under the commercial name "Watersaver." In theory, at least, tall fescue would use half the water of bluegrass and stay green throughout the year, advertising hoopla I readily believed. A few days later, rake and shovel in hand, I set to work leveling the yard.

It didn't take me long to realize that a rake and shovel wouldn't cut it. The soil was studded with rocks, and I'd have spent days removing them by hand. Instead, I rented a tractor with an attachment called a rock hog, a giant rake that scraped and furrowed the earth, removing rocks in the process. A half day's touch-up work with a hand rake produced a relatively flat seedbed, and the next day I spread seventy-five pounds of fescue and ten pounds of bluegrass (the store's recommendation for a quick green-up), rolled it in with a water drum, and set out my sprinklers.

My fescue came up, after an interminable wait, in fits and starts. Not surprisingly, the soil least compacted by the backhoe sprouted the thickest stands, something quite predictable had I thought about it, which I didn't. In two weeks I had green fuzz; in a month the fuzz had retreated into crevices in the soil. Most of the partially shaded backyard didn't take at all, along with half of the front yard and everything along the west side of the foundation. The leftover seed I'd flung in the two aspen groves, unwatered but protected by a moist mat of dead grass and other debris, grew a lawn as thick as the hair on a eunuch.

159

Still, by fall the whole yard was passably green, though a cursory examination revealed numerous flaws. Patches of dirt still lay exposed to the sun and wind, and Russian thistle, a despicable and utterly tenacious weed, was thriving in the bare spots. Had I known how poorly my trees would fare over the winter, I might have taken consolation in growing even those.

Leafless branches respire during the cold months, and although water loss in hardwoods is much less severe than that in pines, it happens. During a typically balmy January of subzero temperatures, humidity drops to nothing, and in dry years water stored in roots is used up. A midwinter watering can save trees, a fact I belatedly realized the following spring, when I viewed the carnage wrought by the previous six months of cold, brittle weather.

Almost to a sapling, my aspens had died. Those few still alive sprouted hard, dry buds, which produced anemic and undersized leaves. They'd had other problems, I learned later; the trees had come from bad stock, and my nurseryman graciously offered to replace them all. But losing a year's work was a blow.

Also wiped out were my Russian olives. Hit hard by hoppers the summer before, many hadn't the reserves to make it through the winter. I pulled up one by its dessicated roots, then threw it away in disgust. Of a dozen, only four were still healthy. I'd seen thousands of Russian olives thriving in untended prairie windbreaks, and these were the last trees I'd expected to go belly up.

All save one of my poor Nanking cherries, another supposedly durable shrub, had completely vanished. Only the tiny

160

sapling I'd planted beyond my aspen grove remained, and it wasn't looking too happy about things.

My windbreak had done somewhat better. The Scotch pines had made it through the winter in fine form and were already showing the bright green candles that precipitated new growth. Some had grown six inches or more their first summer, and several of these would shoot up another foot before the coming season was over. The golden willow cuttings had also survived. Only a half dozen of these failed to produce buds, and since cuttings were free, I wasn't worried about the cost of replacements.

The cottonwood cuttings, on the other hand, never had a chance. Free or not, I didn't want to transplant thirty cuttings every year forever, and I considered buying bare-root stock, which was still cheap compared to potted trees. Cheap trees also jibed with a long-standing personal philosophy: Cheap is always better if it works. Thus, I planned the resurrection of my forest.

Of one thing I was certain: Despite the damage wrought the previous winter, I wasn't ready to give up on my aspen groves. But the dozen replacements I had coming would not create the effect I wanted, which was no less than a wall of verdure fronting my yard. Fortunately, I had propertied friends with acres of wild aspens, and they offered me all the trees I could dig up. Armed with a shovel one afternoon, I set out their ranch.

Aspens sucker voraciously. Saplings sprout from horizontally growing roots, a lifeline of nourishment from mother. Transplanting wild stock is tricky—amputate too much supply root and the sapling will die within a week. A foot of root is minimal, more is insurance against loss.

But this sets a practical limit on sapling size. On a tree head-high or taller, it's hard to dig up enough sucker root to keep it alive. Too, dry roots will kill a sapling as surely as a pair of pruning shears to the crown. I shoved a five-gallon bucket of water into the back of my truck, and after I'd pried two or three saplings from the earth, I'd gather them up, shove them in the bucket, and look for more. Most fit reluctantly, and their springy roots soon pushed them right back out. I wanted the trees badly enough to keep at it, but the suicidal tendencies of the saplings tested my resolve. Later that afternoon, after another few hours of hacking away at the earth in my groves, the last aspen was finally transplanted, soaked in, pruned back, and ready to grow.

Thirty Rocky Mountain junipers, ordered the year before, were planted along the drive. The junipers would be a long-term project, since the twelve-inch saplings might take twenty years to reach head height. But I had to start somewhere, and three-footers, given their glacial growth rate, were horribly expensive. Once in, I good-vibed them at every opportunity.

The profusion of Red Osier dogwoods growing along the river had not escaped my notice. Why not swipe a few for the yard? Dogwoods are water-loving plants, but I figured even my drought-resistant fescue lawn would get enough sprinklings to keep the dogwoods healthy. I spent a cold, wet morning excavating them from a subdivision park, no doubt in violation of covenants.

Compared to dogwoods, transplanting aspens had been

child's play. Dogwoods grow in huge, impenetrable clumps, and it was almost impossible to separate individual plants from the mass of subsurface roots and suckers. I hacked and dug for four hours, and after excavating just six or eight plants I threw in the towel. No bush was worth this. In a dark mood it occurred to me that most probably wouldn't make it through the summer anyway. Several weeks later, my setter puppy proceeded to chew one of the transplanted shrubs back to bare earth. Still, by summer's end, all were limping along. The masticated dogwood, on the other hand, had shown real progress, sprouting a thick stand of new shoots in defiance of all reason.

Straight east of my tiny Manhattan home is a row of silver poplars. These are truly magnificent trees, soaring eighty feet into the clouds, the trunks broader than a man can reach around. The silver undersides of the maple-like leaves flutter in the slightest breeze, and fifteen or twenty feet up, the gray, furrowed bark miraculously transforms to smooth ivory skin. Like all poplars, they grow fast, live hard, and die young.

I wanted some. But nursery stock head-high or taller was too expensive to consider. One morning, during my daily walk, I noticed a dozen saplings growing along the banks of a ditch fronting a nearby home. Just beyond, the mother tree, a modest forty-footer, cast a protective shadow. I asked the owner if he would allow me to dig up a few saplings. I'd replace the displaced soil; I'd be environmentally responsible.

"Hell," he growled, "you can take every damn one of them. I'm tired of mowing them down every spring. And you can have that big one, too. Damn thing sends out a million shoots every year."

I dug up seven, three for the west border of my foundation, two for accent in the aspen grove, and two spares that I planted in the far southeast corner of my lot. I didn't realize until months later that I'd planted the first three too close to the foundation, and by then all were thriving. But I'd be damned if I'd move them now, and I figured that by the time the roots grew large enough to tilt my house on end, I'd be one dead arborist, my ashes flung in a smoky cloud over the East Gallatin River.

The Nanking cherries were replaced once again; once again they all died a few months later, much to the chagrin of my nurseryman, who couldn't understand why I was having such crummy luck. His grew just fine.

But natural mortality was the least of it. That second summer, after torrential rain in May and June, the sun popped out and didn't go away until October. Soil moisture evaporated overnight; July and August were the driest in thirty years.

Luckily, my drip irrigation tape was holding up, having sprung only minor leaks after two years of hard use. I gave my trees an overnight soaking every five days, and those closest to the yard also received overspray from the lawn sprinklers, said lawn finally beginning to fill in. Still, the heat and wind were taking their toll. But the trees probably would have made it had it not been for the grasshoppers.

I was told that 1991 wasn't a particularly bad hopper year over most of the state. But a county extension agent had mentioned "hot spots" here and there, one of which included my subdivision. In fact, my subdivision had become a terrestrial free-fire zone, in which any plant less than knee-high was summarily eaten alive. Hoppers clung to the newly installed siding of my home; bashed themselves senseless against the walls in the living room, though I'd been careful to keep the doors shut; and pinged off the windshield of my truck as I drove up the graveled drive. Leaf by leaf the foliage on my precious trees disappeared into the guts of tobacco-spitting insects. Some trees were completely girdled at ground level; most were scalped. I bought an organic, pathogenic, wheat bran grasshopper bait, using five times the required amount, and then a not-so-organic variation that promised to kill the little creatures in two days. Both worked to a degree, but such was the infestation that battalions of replacements arrived within a week. In desperation, I finally bought a full-blown insecticide, Sevin, to spray on the trees. Would this get into my groundwater, I wondered? My nurseryman cringed, and after that I stopped asking.

But the Sevin seemed to work. Damage had certainly not ceased, but the battle was now in stalemate, and it appeared I'd slowed the onslaught enough to weather the warm months still to come. At that point I was called to Iowa due to my father's ill health, and for some reason I can't fathom to this day, neglected to ask any of the neighbors to water my trees in my absence, which several mentioned after the ensuing catastrophe they would have been happy to do.

When I returned two weeks later my lawn was devastated. The entire yard had turned deathly brown, save those few patches of grass that had developed root systems the summer before. Worse, my trees, already weakened by hoppers, had simply cashed it in. The cottonwoods and golden willows in my windbreak were history. Even some of the pines, weakened by drought, had been eaten. Nearly all the aspen saplings under two feet tall were dead, as were two-thirds of my Russian olives.

But a few of the wild aspens I'd transplanted were miraculously holding on. Several of the Scotch pines would grow another foot that summer, towering above their decapitated neighbors. And my chewed-up dogwood was sending out new shoots faster than the old ones could be eaten back. Next year I'd trim all the dogwoods down to ground level and see what happened. I'd also replant the aspen grove, replacing once more those I'd lost. Into the windbreak would go two new rows of cottonwoods, bare-root stock rather than cuttings this time, and I'd try cotoneaster shrubs for a hedge along the driveway, which are supposedly drought *and* insect resistant.

In October, I planted three burr oaks in the windbreak and, on a whim, stuck a red oak I bought for half price in the grove farthest from the house. If it makes it . . . but no, I'm not going to think about it.

Epilogue: This winter the deer came up and chewed my aspen trees to hell and gone. The red oak was damaged, but it's hanging in there. I sprayed what was left of my saplings with a deer repellent and offered prayers to whatever gods control these things. Don't the deer have enough food down by the river? A week later, I found four of them standing by the back fence, waiting for me to leave. I chased them away and haven't seen them since.

166

A HOME
ON THE RANGE

"What the hell is *that?*" Dan Porter sighted down one wall of my foundation, then walked across the crawl space and stared at the offending corner in disbelief. The foundation jutted from under the rim joist three-quarters of an inch, a mistake I hoped to somehow camouflage with siding. "You use a string on this?"

"What's a string for?"

"Like I showed you. You stretch it out from corner to corner, and then you line the wall up under it. That way it's always perfect."

"Nothing on this house is going to be perfect," I said. I'd been working on my home—my lifelong dream—for two months now, and the one thing I knew, after hours of deciphering the Chinese hieroglyphics printed on blueprints and hammering my fingers flat, was that "perfect" was not within my purview as a carpenter. In fact, I'm not a carpenter, I'm a writer. You heard it here first.

I'd bought the land eighteen months earlier with most of a modest inheritance from my grandmother, then stashed the remaining money in the bank, adding to it in tiny increments, a nearly hopeless attempt at saving the cash I needed to build my own place. One year later, out of the blue, my mother gave me an early inheritance so I could begin building right away. My father, ever the pragmatist, suggested I buy a finished place instead, a suggestion he probably knew I'd ignore. Dad had also once told me that every man wants to build his own home at some point in his life, but few had the time. I had time and little else. I was thirty-four years old.

The next five months were an exciting blur of blueprints, bids on materials, and intense research on energy-efficient housing. I lined up an excavator, priced gravel by the yard, and weighed the pros and cons of various foundation materials. Ultimately, I chose treated plywood, a durable foundation I could build solo. In May I broke ground, and by July the foundation walls were up, built on grade and then dragged, lifted, and sledgehammered into place around the perimeter of the crawl space. By the time I'd nailed on the floor joists and subflooring, temperatures were pushing ninety-five, and at the end of each day I found respite from the heat and dust in the shade under the subfloor, my thoughts still racing, marveling at what I'd done with my own soft and bloodied hands. Every few days Dan would show, chastise my mistakes, then help me correct them. That my house has not tipped on its side is due in part to his help, and also to his favorite maxim, repeated like a refrain upon spying yet another of my boondoggles: "Take your time, do it right."

Around midsummer I began framing the walls. The first to go up was a thirty-footer, the largest in the house. Had I an ounce of common sense, I'd have started with something smaller, less prone to kiting in the wind. I'd borrowed a pair of wall jacks, which operate like giant car jacks: Each is first slid down the length of a vertical twelve- or sixteen-foot two-by-four, then hooked under the top plate of the wall. When the handles are pumped up and down, the device climbs back up the two-by-four, hoisting the top of the wall off the deck a few inches per pump. The wall jack is an example of our lost American ingenuity: a cheap and simple product that will work the way it is supposed to work forever.

The wall went up without a hitch until it was nearly vertical, where it rested in delicate equilibrium, rippling slightly in the breeze. I'd planned for this; I had several two-by-fours stacked nearby, which I used to brace wall to subfloor. Later, the plan went, I'd release the braces one by one, plumbing the wall one yard at a time. What I hadn't planned for was the next gust of wind, which ballooned out the wall like air fills a ship's sail, instantly ripping out my braces and sending all thirty feet of wall reeling backwards off the deck, with me clinging to a window opening in a puny attempt to wrestle hundreds of pounds of plywood and raw lumber back in place. Just when it appeared it would go off the edge and topple squarely over the temporary power pole, crushing my arms and torching the foundation and subfloor in a tower of flames, the wind eased, and the wall groaned and sagged back, teetering precariously just where I wanted it. I raced up and down its length nailing on every spare brace I had, then scavenged the yard for more, until the wall sprouted two-by-fours like a rowing shell sprouts oars.

This was going to be fun. In fact, I'd told my father as much during our last talk because, in the course of our conversation, he'd asked me if I was still having fun; and the very next day I stepped off the deck and onto a sixteen-penny nail that sank through the sole of my tennis shoe and an inch into my right foot. I hopped around on my unpunctured foot for ten minutes, swearing at my own stupidity and cursing the world. My Irish temper.

By July, the deck of my home was like an open oven. Heat waves shimmied above the subfloor, and sweat poured from my brow, flushing sunscreen into my burning eyes and drenching my already filthy T-shirt. I drank water by the gallon and craved more. Despite the heat, the remaining exterior walls on the first floor went up smoothly, though the last was hammered in place with a sledgehammer. It was then I realized how much the house was out of level; a marble placed on the northwest corner of the subfloor would have rolled kitty-corner across the length of it. I'd built the foundation on a gravel footer, standard procedure for a wood foundation. But a concrete footer, I now realized, would have given me a solid and far more level platform on which to raise walls. My 20/20 hindsight would be a depressingly recurring theme for the next two years. Despite the books I read and the hundreds of questions I asked, a better way would often dawn on me only after the project in question was finished.

My home is divided into two parts: A twelve- by thirty-three-foot box enclosing the two downstairs bedrooms adjoins an eighteen- by thirty-three-foot box that houses the living room, dining room, and kitchen. Above the dining room and kitchen is the second-floor master bedroom, with its own private bath and sauna, and a balcony open to the living room below. The walls flanking the balcony are eighteen feet high. After erecting all the exterior downstairs walls with problems only on the initial thirty-footer, I was nearly killed by the first balcony wall.

The bottom plate of a two-by-four wall is customarily toenailed to the subfloor before the wall is raised. But I'd used eight-penny, not sixteen-penny nails to toenail the bottom plate, assuming they'd hold the weight of the lumber and plywood extending above the jack, which of necessity I'd positioned only halfway up the wall. When I'd jacked the wall two-thirds of the way up the bottom plate kicked out, and the wall, teetering for an instant on the fulcrum created by the

jack, came rushing down at me. I dove off the deck a fraction
of a second before the whole thing crashed with a tremendous
roar, shattering the wall and sending a shower of splinters
flying into the yard.

Because of my own carelessness, nearly a hundred dollars
of good lumber had been utterly ruined. I went into a scream-
ing rage, and looking for something to throttle, spied my
hammer lying among the tools flung from my tool belt. I threw
it as far as I could. I had pitched some as a kid; the hammer
thudded down close to my back property line. It wasn't until
an hour later, when I finally calmed enough to think ratio-
nally, that I realized how close I'd come to ending my carpen-
try career in a welter of kiln-dried pine and waferboard. Years
ago, in Wyoming, I'd run into a bartender named Kenny.
Kenny had been a roughneck until some iron fell on him; now
he walked funny and worked in a bar. With a rebuilt knee,
trick ankle, and chronically sore back, I walk plenty funny
already, and it chilled me to think of what could have hap-
pened.

Later, a small bearing wall on one side of the kitchen fell
around my shoulders, but I was able to catch it halfway down.
At that point, relieved that I'd saved the lumber, I let it slide
from my hands, directly onto my foot. The wall then broke in
half. I managed to scrape together some friends for the up-
stairs walls, and they went up in a day, smooth as a baby's
bottom.

Over the years, I've made it a habit to visit Norm and Sil
Strung every few weeks, usually just prior to dinner. Norm
was an inspiration to a lot of writers in the valley, one of a

handful of free-lancers who had made it. He and his wife Sil had built themselves a home twenty years earlier, and I leaned heavily on both of them for advice. But in the spring of '91, when the two returned from their winter home in Mexico, Norm was a sick man.

Because of my busy schedule, I didn't see him until a couple of weeks later, in June. "It's some kind of goddamn hiatus hernia," he said. He tapped his chest with his finger and puffed on a cigarette. "The doctors in Salt Lake want to see me again. That means we're gonna have to drive all the way over there just when the fishing around here is picking up." Sil fussed over a roast on the kitchen counter, preparing another gargantuan meal for the nonstop stream of guests the two hosted.

Norm *looked* well enough; pale, but fit. He'd lost weight—said he hadn't had much of an appetite in Mexico that year—but he'd been a bit overweight anyway. They were leaving for Salt Lake in a week, and over after-dinner drinks I told them I'd see them when they got back. Norm told me he'd do what he could to help with my house, depending on how he felt. I said I'd be happy to rototill his garden while he was gone, an offer I make every year and one they've yet to take me up on. Thus am I generous with my time and labor.

But within a week my promise was all but forgotten. I called the Strungs upon their return, found all was well, and immersed myself in my work, shrugging off reports from friends that Norm was still ailing. I didn't visit the two of them again until August, though I spoke with both on the phone several times.

*   *   *

The previous fall, after raising the walls, I'd begun shingling the roof. The exposed walls and subflooring had spent six months soaking up rainwater, and I'd been anxious to protect the thousands of dollars of wood I'd sawed and hammered in place, particularly the subfloor, which had begun to swell at the seams. Unfortunately, on the day I chose to start, it was snowing. I couldn't believe my rotten luck. Snow-covered plywood is slick as otter skin, and the steep pitch on my roof made it a death trap. I was forced to postpone my start until the next day, when most of the three inches of new snow had melted.

But by the following morning, the wet plywood had frozen solid, glazing the roof with a layer of ice. I climbed up a ladder with a shovel in hand, intending to scrape off the rime as best I could, but it was a hopeless task, and I was forced to climb down and wait once more for the sun to warm things.

At noon I tried again. After gaining the main roof I crawled to the ridge, straddling it. I don't recall what I stepped on—perhaps a patch of ice or simply a wet spot—but an instant later I was careering down the roof on my back, flying briefly through the air to the bedroom roof below, then rocketing toward the eave and a short but unpleasant descent through space. Here, however, the sun had completely dried out the wood, and I skidded to a stop a foot or two before dropping off the edge. It had happened so quickly I hadn't had time to think, and now that it was over I was curiously absent of emotion, feeling neither fear nor relief, but rather, resigned to finishing the job at hand.

The roof took five more days. Each night it snowed; each morning the sun melted the accumulation just enough by noon

175

to coat the roof with ice the following morning. I was finally forced to rope myself to the ridge top, bouncing across the pitch like a rock climber, shingles in one hand and a nail gun in the other. On the last day, Dan arrived to help me nail off the porch. After installing twenty-five squares of shingles without a major mistake, I seriously miscalculated two rows, exposing a jagged, three-foot gap of black adhesive directly under the upstairs picture window, where it was plainly visible for public comment. Dan, with his usual tact, wanted to know what the hell I'd done *there.*

"I screwed up. I didn't do it on purpose," I said.

"Sometimes I wonder."

"I'll bet."

Several months later, in what should have been the dead of winter, it rained. To my immense disappointment, I discovered that my new roof leaked like a sieve. Rivulets of water ran from the walls and puddled on the subfloor, and near the back door and downstairs bedrooms miniature lakes had formed. I couldn't believe water was coming through the shingles, but then, where else would it be coming from? Despite the work involved, shingling a roof is straightforward: One simply staples down roofing felt and nails overlapping shingles on top of it. How could I have messed up?

That night, I sought in vain for answers. Leaks are almost impossible to trace, even on a completely exposed roof. Part of the problem was undoubtedly the openings for windows. Although every opening save two was covered by at least a thirty-inch overhang, wind-driven spray still managed to find a way inside. My biggest worry, however, was the seam where the roof on the west side of the house met the wall on the east side. On the subfloor directly below, a linear lake thirty feet long had formed, though the roof-to-wall connection above was ostensibly watertight. The next morning I clambered up the roof for a closer look. I found I'd neglected to trim the roofing felt jutting from under the shingles bordering the seam, and the felt, in effect, had created an elongated funnel, trapping water draining down the sides of the sheathing. I trimmed it back, caulked it closed, and hoped the siding that would eventually cover the walls would take care of the problem once and for all. To my surprise, that is what happened, and all but a minor leak under the back door disappeared once the siding was up.

That April was as miserable as February had been balmy. I'd bought two thousand board feet of beveled cedar siding, and I spent several days staining it in intermittent rain, a monumental mistake. Applying stain in the rain is so widely recognized as unworkable that even the paint store owner, knowing I was a rank novice, hadn't warned against it, erroneously assuming that I knew better. The upshot was two thousand board feet of expensive wood with a cheap paint job. Nevertheless, I was determined to put the siding up, for once up, I was essentially through with the outside of the house. There would be endless hours of trim work still remaining, but that could wait until after I'd moved in.

The rain eased for a few days at the start of the project, enough for me to finish one small quarter of the south half of the house. Since I'd picked through the cedar and used only unblemished wood, it looked fine. But the west side of the house, on which I'd used up the remaining wood I'd ruined the week before, looked terrible. Applying another coat of stain made the blemishes darker and less noticeable, but noticeable nonetheless.

Because of the strain of making a living concurrent with building a house, my social life, such as it was, had ground to a dead lull. Yet, in keeping with a pattern consistent throughout my life, once I stopped looking, opportunity was thrown in my lap. A week into the siding project, I was called by a woman introduced to me earlier by a mutual friend. She owned a local manufacturing business, and wondered what I'd charge to write a story promoting her company. I had no idea what to charge, and wasn't really sure I could find a magazine willing to run such a piece. That was okay, she told me; we'd work on the idea some more, and, in the meantime, would I be interested in dinner?

K. was a raven-haired beauty of nearly forty, but her lithe build and unlined face erased a decade from her true age. Perhaps because of my red hair and ultra-fair skin, I'm a helpless pushover for exotic, tanned women, and K. was certainly that: Her dark hair, dark eyes, and high cheekbones gave her an Italian or Latin look, I couldn't decide which. Much later I learned that her immediate relatives were actually Polish. But an unknown and distant ancestor had been Aztec, and in the curious miracle of genetics, that nearly lost strain of Indian blood had manifested in her.

We saw each other two or three times. One night, I took her to a dance, and by night's end I'd sensed a change. That evening I asked her out again, but no, business was pressing, and would be indefinitely. All right, I'd been around enough to take a hint. It had been fun while it lasted. I didn't call her back, and assumed I'd never hear from her again. For a long time, I didn't.

Meanwhile, I was so busy installing siding I spent only a day or two dealing with my disappointment. In order to finish the towering north wall of my house, I'd borrowed pump jacks from a friend, devices that act much the same as wall jacks. A pump jack is slid down a vertical pole made of nailed-together two-by-fours and, like a wall jack, climbs the pole when the handle is pumped. A jack and a pole are attached to either side of a wall, usually by nailing a gusset from pole to roof. Scaffolding is suspended between the jacks, creating a work platform. But such platforms are notoriously unstable and sway and lurch in the slightest breeze.

The wind howled throughout April, driving rain and sleet into my face and down my neck. Walking about on the swaying scaffolding terrified me, and handling the twelve- and sixteen-foot lengths of siding only made matters worse. At least once every day, the wind caught a board broadside, instantly tearing it from my hands. One afternoon, still clutching a board I was determined not to lose, a gust nearly sent me spinning fifteen feet to the ground below.

After several near falls and days of wet misery, I finished the north side of the house only to discover I'd run out of siding, with the east side of my home still unfinished. I couldn't afford more of the same cedar I'd used on the rest of the place, so instead bought several hundred feet of cedar from a cut-rate dealer west of town. I got what I paid for: lousy wood at a good price. Since I'd learned by then not to stain siding in the rain, it looked presentable once up, though the hundreds of knots contrasted with the relatively clear wood elsewhere. Still, by then I didn't care. I was so relieved it was over, so utterly happy that I would never, ever have to nail up another board, that it could have turned purple for all I cared. As far as I was concerned the outside of the house was finished. From here on in I'd concentrate on making the inside livable.

Building a poorly insulated, drafty home in a state where January lows burst engine blocks strikes me as the height of stupidity, yet to this day that is exactly how most are built. Energy-efficient construction takes extra time, and here as elsewhere, time is money. Never mind that sensible, efficient construction makes for a more comfortable home summer and winter and saves cash in the long run.

Example: Since wall studs conduct or "bridge" heat from the inside of a house to the outside, my plans called for double walls, a nonbearing interior stud wall built twelve inches inside the outside, bearing wall. The space between the two would be filled with overlapping batts of fiberglass insulation, eliminating thermal bridging.

To my pleasant surprise, the interior walls, save the expansive south gable in the living room, went up smoothly. Minus the sheathing I'd nailed on the exterior walls, most were light enough that I could lift them in place myself, tacking them to the trusses above. The gable wall presented a problem only because eight- to twelve-foot studs had to be positioned on an eight-foot wall already in place below, then nailed one by one to the trusses above, twenty-plus feet off the floor.

By July I'd finished, sheathed out the twelve-inch-wide perimeter around the windows and doors with waferboard, installed the windows, and was ready to wire and plumb the interior. I'd been looking forward to Norm Strung's annual Fourth of July party, but Sil had canceled that year's event, since Norm wasn't recuperating as she had hoped, and she feared the typical Strung blowout would be too much for him. This set off no alarms as perhaps it should have; Norm was tough and I figured he'd shake off whatever was bothering him in a few more weeks. Still, I decided to pay the Strungs another visit. But a scant few days afterwards, before I had a chance to see them, I received a solemn call from my mother. My father was very sick. Could I drive home right away?

Dad died in his sleep an hour after I arrived home, before I could say good-bye. He'd had what amounted to a heart attack a year earlier, and his health had declined steadily since then. When I'd spoken to him last, he'd mumbled only a few words—no mention of my house, which had always interested him—before turning the phone over to my mother.

We hadn't always been close. I was an emotional but headstrong and independent kid, my strongest legacy from my father the quick temper that curses every member of our family. Yet over many years we had, if not worked out our disagreements, at least reached an unspoken truce: We'd try to avoid arguing during the few days every year we spent together. Dad was fiercely proud of my determination to build my own place. More than anything, I'd have liked him there when I finished it.

Back in Montana, I tried to find enthusiasm for the upcoming wiring job. I pored over the diagrams of switch connections in a book I'd purchased prior to taking a home wiring

181

course the year before. The course had been a waste of money—I was too bored to apply myself—but now I wished I'd paid more attention. The diagrams in the book were completely undecipherable. I finally gave up and ran the wiring anyway. I'd get a friend to show me the switch connections later.

The plumbing was something else again. I'd spent days studying how-to books, and though I had an inkling of the theory behind plumbing (there *is* a reason your toilets work), I had no idea what local codes would require, how to sweat copper water lines, or how to cut and install PVC drain pipes.

Luckily, I was a few dollars ahead, thanks to my obsession with buying lumber on sale and substituting used materials for new whenever possible. I decided to hire my friend Rick, an experienced plumber, to moonlight my place in his spare time. Aside from the excavation of my foundation and well, it was the only work I hired out on the entire house.

To keep costs down, I helped Rick sand and clean joints, cutting him the lengths of pipe he needed. I was amazed at his efficiency. We accomplished in three days what I'm sure would have taken me at least as many weeks. Still, there were the inevitable snafus. One day he handed me a "hole hog," suggesting I use it to drill parallel holes through several wall studs prior to installation of a vent pipe. "Keep your eye on that thing, Dave," he said. "It'll bite you."

A hole hog is a monstrous two-handed drill designed to bore holes from two to four inches in diameter. I placed the bit firmly against a stud, braced my legs, and pushed the trigger. An instant later the drill was skipping across the room and I was staring in disbelief at the blood spattered on the wall opposite me. Then my fingers: The bit had jumped out of the hole and run across the knuckles of my left hand, slicing the skin on my middle finger to bare muscle. Blood poured from the wound and dripped on the floor.

I walked out from under the balcony, dazed and staring in morbid fascination at my hand. I called upstairs to Rick. "I've got a problem here," I said. "I cut my fingers pretty good with that goddamn drill back there."

"How bad is it?"

"I don't know. You might have to take me in for stitches. I'm bleeding all over the fucking floor."

Rick came down and examined my wound. "Oooh," he said. "I'll bet that feels good. You want to go to town?"

"Let me think about this for a moment. You got bandages or something?"

"I've got some Band-Aids in the truck, but all they'll do is hold the skin together. You're gonna need stitches or something."

I'd been among America's uninsured for nearly a decade, too chronically broke to afford health insurance of any kind. Finally, a couple of years earlier, I'd managed to scrape up funds for what amounted to a catastrophic policy designed to keep me solvent in case of life-threatening injury or illness. A visit to the doctor would cost hundreds of dollars I didn't have and my high-deductible policy wouldn't cover.

"Let's put on the Band-Aids, and I'll see if Scott has some tape," I said. Scott, my next-door neighbor, did have tape, as well as sterile gauze, which he cheerfully wound around my fingers and taped in place.

Surprisingly, the cuts were never painful. With three of my

fingers immobilized, my left hand was next to useless, but I'm a right-hander anyway. When I took off the bandages at the end of the week, the wounds had knit together nicely.

A few days later, my well driller made the final connection between well and house, then helped me hook up the pressure tank. When I flipped on the power, the water lines cracked and banged, the pressure tank cycled on, and then all was silent. "Do you think it works?" I asked.

The driller grinned and turned on a hose bib. After a blast of spray coughed out, water gushed on the lawn in a steady stream. I was still smiling when he left.

By the time I called in another friend, Kent Porter, for an impromptu wiring inspection, I was feeling good about my progress, though I'd been working on the house over a year and had accomplished only half of what I'd hoped. The wiring and plumbing were essentially complete, and the exterior of the house needed only touch-up work with a caulk gun to make it weathertight. The windows and doors had been set for months, and though I was still lacking insulation, Sheetrock, a kitchen, the finished wood floor, and trim—in short, everything that would make the house livable—my imagination was months ahead of schedule. My home would be small but warm and sunny, a place, I hoped, that would be a focal point for friends and family: Dave's place.

I thought I'd be completely finished in a few more months, but Kent, a professional carpenter who had built himself a superinsulated home several years earlier, had sobering news. Working solo, it would take me as long to complete the

interior as it had to finish everything else that had gone be-
fore. My heart sank. "That will be another year!" I wailed.
Kent laughed. "You'll see," he said.

A week later I stopped at a bakery in town and was relax-
ing on a bench outside when a green Subaru pulled up. K.
bounced out and, spying me, slid onto the bench beside me,
opening the conversation with a story about her puppy,
which, while running alongside the Subaru, had severed an
artery and nearly died. K. had been en route to my place.

I'd forgotten all about her, and found it amazing she hadn't
forgotten me. We chatted for a few minutes before she left,
leaving me completely bewildered by the visit. Why such at-
tentiveness now, when, six months earlier, she couldn't find
time for another date? I finally shrugged it off to her innate
friendliness and had about convinced myself of that when,
several weeks later, she showed up at the house. The follow-
ing week, she stopped by again.

She was always cordial, always talkative; but after a few
minutes of conversation, she'd excuse herself and head for
town. Normally, I'd have lost little time asking her out—it's
not like women make nuisances of themselves around me—
but having already been put off once, I was a bit gun-shy.

I decided to shelve the K. question and get on with my
work. Now that the wiring and plumbing were in, I could
install the insulation, a task I'd been dreading for months.

When I was a child, my mother had mistakenly washed my
clothes with our living room's fiberglass curtains. The upshot
was a tortured two-day vacation from school while I scratched

myself raw. I had nearly three times the insulation in my small home as in that of a comparably sized house, which meant three times the exposure. Consequently, to lessen penetration of glass particles into the pores of my skin, I dusted my wrists and neck with talcum powder and wore two shirts, a dust mask, and goggles. Then I buttoned the sleeves of my outer shirt over a pair of cotton gloves, sealing the wrists with masking tape.

It worked for awhile. For the first few days I was reasonably comfortable, but toward the end of the week those parts of my body closely bound by clothing—my waist, neck, and wrists—started to itch. Still, I found that an immediate shower and generous use of hand lotion on the affected areas kept my discomfort minimal.

Insulating the cathedral ceiling made matters far worse. In order to reach it, I'd borrowed three tiers of scaffolding from Kent, and by late July, the temperature just under the roof, which radiated heat absorbed by the shingles directly into the house, must have been over a hundred degrees. Every third batt I wedged in loosened and slumped to the floor, and I howled with rage each time it happened. The placement of each batt had to be just so; voids meant possible convection currents and a subsequent loss of heat. A minute loss perhaps, but I was going to do this one thing right if it killed me.

Once the last of the batts were in, I covered the insulation with a vapor barrier, a sheet of six-mil plastic stapled to every interior wall and ceiling in the house. This made the place virtually airtight, for which I received no end of grief from numerous friends who assured me a that house had to "breathe" in order to prevent condensation. In fact, however, a well-constructed, tight home with a controlled ventilation system (which I'd already installed) is much more efficient than a home that breathes via poorly sealed windows and doors.

I sealed the vapor barrier with Tremco Acoustical Sealant, a black, permanently soft caulk that is as effective at creating an airtight seal as it is impossible to remove from your face and hands. Once, after discovering to my dismay that I'd rubbed Tremco into my hair, I spent fifteen minutes trying to wash it out with a gasoline-soaked cloth, then spent the rest of the afternoon praying my head wouldn't combust when I walked by a sunny window.

There are a thousand and one details involved in building a house, and between the time I installed the vapor barrier and covered it with Sheetrock, the details kept me occupied for days. Exposed plumbing and wiring had to be covered and protected from wayward drywall screws, and nailers—blocks of wood to which the drywall is attached—had to be nailed in an impossible number of nooks and crannies. During all these projects the vapor barrier was torn and repaired, then torn and repaired again. Seams were resealed for the umpteenth time, and the bottom plates of walls were given a final caulking to the subfloor. Outlet boxes were filled with airtight expanding foam.

Finally, though, I finished the prep work and planned on hanging drywall the following Saturday. I'd organized a "Sheetrock party" to help, the deal being that I'd supply food and booze if a whole lot of my friends would show up for the weekend and at least help me get the ceilings hung, a task I couldn't do by myself. Come Saturday, exactly one person showed, about par for the course. Two hours later, a couple more arrived.

I wasn't surprised. Anyone who enjoys hanging Sheetrock needs a quick dose of fresh air, and everyone I'd invited had hung more of it than I. But, lacking experience, I'd overestimated the help I'd need. The four of us hung most of the ceilings in a morning, and I took the rest of a long week to put up the walls myself—far less of a chore than I'd imagined. In fact, the worst part of the job was driving drywall screws. I'd tacked the corners of each sheet in place with nails, then returned and driven in screws at twelve-inch intervals. Every half hour or so I'd get sloppy and miss a stud, my bad aim manifest the instant the screw spun with no resistance, boring a neat hole in my precious vapor barrier. It infuriated me that there was nothing I could do. At first I yanked the screws out and filled the holes with caulk, but by the end of the week I left the damn things in there. Let 'em spin.

I finished taping the seams in early September, a summer forfeited to almost daily work on my home. On one of my rare free evenings, I paid a long overdue visit to the Strungs, whom I had not seen since May. Sil flung open the massive pine door of their cabin and gave me a hug, a greeting I've come to expect and always look forward to. I followed her into the kitchen, poured myself a drink from Norm's scotch, and took a seat at the kitchen table. Another couple wandered in and introduced themselves. The Strungs are forever entertaining friends.

Sil wanted to know how my house was coming. Would I be moving in soon?

Possibly by Christmas, I told her, maybe January. Maybe

February, even. I'd been wrong on every projection so far, and there was no reason to think I'd be right on this one.

"How's Norm doing?" I asked. "Is he around?"

"He's in the den," Sil said.

I chatted with Sil a few more minutes, then walked into the den. Norm was sitting on the couch, sipping a drink and watching a football game.

He'd lost a tremendous amount of weight. His jeans hung from his emaciated frame, and he'd taken his belt to the last notch. I'd never seen him so frail. But he grinned up at me, nodding at the seat beside him.

"How are you Norm? Looks like you've lost some weight."

Norm paused. "I've got cancer, pal. And I'm afraid it's terminal."

That was Norm, to tell me like that, straight from the shoulder.

I spent the next thirty minutes in a fog of disbelief. Norm made small talk; I remember little of it. I do remember he'd decided not to opt for chemotherapy. What was the point? He'd had a good life and although he hadn't planned on heading out so soon, he had no regrets. Three weeks later he walked up the trout stream he and Sil had lived on for twenty-five years—nearly half his life—and shot himself. While all in the valley mourned the following morning, I cried in the shower, where no one could hear me.

By fall my house was, if not racing toward completion, at least moving at a faster clip than at any time since the initial excavation, eighteen months earlier. I textured and painted the walls in two days, inhaling enough paint and dust in the process to give me a minor smoker's cough. The new paint gleamed pearly white, instantly transforming the interior. The house now shone with sunlight to the very back of the kitchen, and I marveled at the change.

Next I laid up tongue-and-groove knotty pine on the ceilings I'd not covered with Sheetrock. The dining room, kitchen, and upstairs bedroom went up quickly, without a tantrum on my part. But once again the cathedral ceiling gave me fits. Rather than piece it together with short and easy-to-handle lengths of wood, I used full-length, twelve-foot boards, and each had warped enough to make untroubled installation impossible. Consequently, I wedged, pried, and hammered them in place, tore the vapor barrier repeatedly, and cooked in the intense heat two feet below the apex of the ceiling. One day, enraged at tearing yet another hole in the vapor barrier, I scrambled down the scaffolding to the floor, grabbed the board I'd flung down ahead of me, and smashed it to splinters against the steel rungs of the scaffolding ladder. In the aftermath, of course, I felt sheepish but relieved. Fortunately for me, my friends are largely unaware of these Jekyll-Hyde transformations, for nobody likes being labeled a jerk.

Earlier that year, I'd bought a truckload of tongue-and-groove fir flooring on sale, then had it delivered to the job site. I moved all thirty-five hundred lineal feet of it inside the house, three boards at a time. The pile seriously reduced my usable floor space, but there was nowhere else to put it. Now, finally, I could install it and get it out of the way.

Unlike the pine in the ceilings, my fir flooring was straight and almost clear, an even better grade of wood than I'd suspected when I bought it. The installation was straightforward and time-consuming, but there were no serious glitches, and five days later I had a finished, if unvarnished, floor. For the first time in eighteen months of hard and largely tedious work, my home looked livable. I still needed a kitchen and bathroom, miles of trim, fixtures, heat, and lights, but I was getting there, and I found myself musing over potential dates of completion.

A few days later, K. dropped in for another chat. The following evening, Denver Bryan, a friend hosting me for dinner, gazed across his kitchen table in pity and wonder. "You haven't asked her out *yet?* What does she have to do?"

"Well, we went out once before, and you know how that went." Etc. etc.

"She's acting just like a doe around a buck, Dave. She's interested, but you have to make the first move." Denver has a master's degree in wildlife biology, and these analogies please him.

But I knew he was right, so the following week I called her and suggested lunch. She agreed to meet me at a local burger joint. The conversation flowed. We made a date for a movie two nights later, and the following night, dinner at her place. Then dinner at mine. No boyfriend, she said.

After it's over, you remember the little things—an arm linked through yours, a look. But during the next two weeks I couldn't imagine why we hadn't clicked all those months before. Still, my rapidly melting reserve was tempered by concrete reality: I had a house to build before I ran out of money. I wanted to spend as much time with K. as possible, but she was at least as busy as I was, with two demanding businesses and a life of her own.

191

*　　*　　*

Among those who have never built a house, there's a misconception that the walls and roof, constituting the bulk of the structure, are the hardest to build. But anyone who's been there will tell you otherwise. Framing is straightforward. And the shingles, siding, windows, and doors—all the things that finish off the exterior of a house—can be put up in a couple of weeks with a good crew. It's the construction from the outside in that wears on you.

Unfortunately, the closer you get to completion, the more painstaking the work becomes. Installing insulation is not fun, but laying, taping, and painting the drywall that goes over it is worse. I've already described wooden ceilings. Stairways aren't complicated but are nearly impossible to get right on the first try.

The most time-consuming of all are kitchen cabinets, which is why most owner/builders buy them ready-made. But even cheap, laminated particleboard cabinets in the quantity needed for my kitchen would have cost upwards of twelve hundred dollars, and modest units—with oak doors and panels, for instance—would have been two thousand dollars or more.

I simply didn't have that kind of money. Already I was forecasting a deficit, knowing I'd run out of funds before the house was complete. For three to four hundred dollars I could build the cabinets myself, and the money saved might be enough to finish off a bedroom and bath. I'd still have to buy panels, but I'd get birch, not oak; and I could rip leftover fir flooring for the facing. Panels hidden by the dishwasher, range, and refrigerator would be sturdy ACX plywood. The cabinet doors would be tongue-and-groove pine, cheap and rustic, like almost everything else in the house.

My first screwup nearly stopped the project before it began. There are standard heights for everything in a house: thirty-one inches for a bathroom vanity, twenty-nine for tables, thirty for handrails. Kitchen countertops are thirty-six inches high and twenty-four inches wide. They've always been that way; it's a standard in the industry.

Somehow, after months of studying the plans for my home, I'd failed to note the height of the kitchen counter, printed in plain English in at least three different locations on my blueprints. I assumed it was thirty-three inches high, and when I wired in the appliance outlets, I installed them thirty-seven inches off the floor, adding four inches for good measure. That purely arbitrary four inches spared a tremendously expensive repair job. Had I installed the outlets an inch lower, I'd have had to rip through the Sheetrock, vapor barrier, and insulation to reposition them, then seal the entire wall up again.

Even at thirty-seven inches, I realized to my dismay that the appliance outlets would rest directly on top of the counter, rather than several inches above them, as is standard. This wasn't a huge problem, nor even against code. It simply looked amateurish, and the kitchen was the one place I'd hoped to showcase my very minor skills as a craftsman. Since I like to cook, I'd thought out the kitchen more than any other room in the house. That I could have overlooked something as basic as countertop height numbed me. I decided to make the countertops thirty-five and a half inches, which would give me about a quarter inch of space beneath each outlet cover. Not perfect, but the best I could do under the circumstances.

Cabinet construction took roughly a month and a half, for once not far off my estimate. Panels were placed, plumbed, and nailed into ledgers anchored to the wall, then faced with strips of fir flooring one and a half inches wide. Thin strips of fir were screwed to the inside of the panels to support shelving, which was later dropped in place and tacked down. Once the base cabinets were roughed in, three-quarter-inch particleboard was glued and nailed over the top, creating a solid platform for the off-white Formica that would form the finished surface of the counter.

By the time the base cabinets were complete, I'd gained enough confidence to tackle the slightly more complicated wall cabinets above. These I built on a pair of sawhorses in the living room, one cabinet per day. Each following morning, each cabinet was propped in place and attached to wall studs with three-inch Sheetrock screws.

One afternoon, as I ripped one of the final lengths of facing on a radial arm saw, the board slipped away from the fence and instantly kicked back into my hand. I cursed, shut off the saw, and examined my hand. A wedge of wood half an inch wide and four inches long had completely pierced the flesh on the heel of my right hand, along with another, smaller splinter that had plunged to bone directly below the knuckle of my index finger. I walked to the edge of the porch and sat down, trying to think above my anger. I yanked on the largest splinter, but it wouldn't budge. I couldn't believe this had happened to me again, so close to completion of the last major project in the house.

Finally, I found a pair of wire clippers, clipped off the largest splinter just above the wound, and jerked it out of my

194

hand with a pair of pliers. After poking around the hole in my knuckle with the tweezers from my Swiss army knife, I located the smaller splinter and yanked that out too. Save for a persistent but minor ache, my hand healed nicely by the end of the week, and after missing a day's work, I finished the installation of the cabinets, careful to keep the blood that seeped from my bandages off the woodwork. When the last cabinet had been hung, the fir trim was given a coat of stain and allowed to dry.

The cabinet doors took several more days. Construction should have been simple. The t&g pine boards were hammered together with a rubber mallet, then braced with strips of fir that formed a backwards z, similar to those on barn doors. Black Sheetrock screws, which I left exposed, secured bracing to pine.

But by the time I'd cut each to size, rounded its edges, installed hinges, and hung it, I found I could build only two or three in half a day. I was still writing every morning, trying to scrape together enough magazine work to stay afloat while I finished the house. Consequently, what should have been three days' work stretched to nearly a week, not counting drawers, which added another two days. When finally I installed the Formica countertop, decorative wood border, and splashguard, Christmas had come and gone. I sank a used (and free) sink in the counter and carted in used appliances bought from friends. The next day, I discovered that the water lines under the sink leaked, but after two hours' work I got that down to a manageable drop or two per hour.

Meanwhile, K. had been stopping by and praising my work, which very much pleased me. I'd been seeing more of her, at her suggestion as much as mine, and against my own cynical judgment had even allowed myself an occasional optimistic thought. Maybe, just maybe, this one wouldn't blow up in my face. Maybe it was about time.

I have this recurring vision of a girls' finishing school: A woman draped in virginal white stands before a class of sixteen-year-olds. One alabaster hand clutches a gleaming, six-inch dagger, and standing directly opposite her, though slashed to ribbons, is what is obviously a male dummy. The woman slides in close, slips her free hand around the dummy's neck, then deftly thrusts the dagger into its solar plexus. "All right, girls," she says, "thrust and rip. All the way to the sternum! Now, repeat after me: We can still be friends!"

Several days prior to finishing the kitchen, K. invited me over for an afternoon football game. The Broncos were in the playoffs, and since we had both lived in Colorado, we both hoped they'd go to the Superbowl. It didn't happen, but that's what we hoped.

I offered to cook a postgame pheasant dinner, and she told me she'd rented movies for the evening. I thought we'd make a night of it.

She spent most of the game on the phone. A week earlier she'd had a breast biopsy, a procedure that probably scared me more than her, and though she was fine, a drove of concerned friends and relatives needed reassurance. While she chatted, I tried to keep track of my two dogs, which I'd brought over to play with her puppy. After introductions, the three went their separate ways, mine less interested in playing than in methodically destroying the dog toys scattered around K.'s backyard. The Broncos won in a squeaker.

A few minutes later, K. slid onto the couch beside me and told me she'd decided she didn't want a commitment, because relationships never worked, and there was too much else going on in her life right now.

Stunned, I stared at the television. What had I done this time?

I hadn't done anything, she told me. Nothing had changed. But she'd been "seeing" this other guy—not seriously, in fact, he was so inconsequential she wished she hadn't brought him up—but anyway, seeing him made her realize she couldn't have a relationship. Not with me. She felt terrible about it, but that's the way it was.

I walked numbly to my car with the dogs scampering around my legs and the half-thawed pheasant under my arm. A week of examining every nuance of that last conversation, of sleepless, thrashing nights, brought little relief. In time, as always, I simply stopped looking for answers.

My house will stand forever. There is baseboard to install and carpet to lay, and the upstairs fixtures are still in boxes on the upstairs floor. Someday, not far from now, when the trim and the carpet are down, and the wainscoting and the closet shelves and all the rest are in place once and for all, my house will become my home, the place I built with my own scarred and calloused hands. Today my house belongs only to me, but, like all dreams, it will live on past me, in the care of others. I hope they know what they're getting.

197